# OGDEN NASH
### has written mad,
#### sad, witty and brilliant
##### verse for thirty years.

§ He was born in 1902 in Rye, New York, and graduated from St. George's School at Newport, Rhode Island, but not from Harvard, which he left at the end of his freshman year. § Having failed to make his fortune in Wall Street in two years, he got a job writing advertising copy for street-car cards. In 1925 he joined the advertising department of Doubleday, Page and Company, Inc. "In the clear and rested ease of 3 P.M.," Christopher Morley reminisces, "when everyone supposed he was doing copy and layout for next month's publications, he was writing the earliest of his metrical outrages." § In 1931 Mr. Nash joined the editorial staff of *The New Yorker,* where he served the customary three months' term. Since leaving the staff, but not the pages of *The New Yorker,* Mr. Nash has devoted his entire time to writing.

The verses in this edition were selected from *Verses from 1929 On,* published by Little, Brown & Company, Inc., at $5.95.

*The*
*Pocket*
*Book*
*of*

# ogden nash

*Introduction by*
*Louis Untermeyer*

PUBLISHED BY POCKET BOOKS · NEW YORK

THE POCKET BOOK OF OGDEN NASH

*Verses from 1929 On* published by
Little, Brown & Company, Inc. in 1959

POCKET BOOK edition published July, 1962
8th printing...........May, 1973

This POCKET BOOK® edition contains a generous selection of verse which
originally appeared in *Verses from 1929 On.* It is printed from brand-new
plates made from completely reset, clear, easy-to-read type.
POCKET BOOK editions are published by Pocket Books, a division of
Simon & Schuster, Inc., 630 Fifth Avenue, New York, N.Y. 10020.
Trademarks registered in the United States and other countries.

L

*For Frances—*
*then, now, and always*

How these curiosities
would be quite forgott,
did not such idle fellowes
as I am putt them downe.

JOHN AUBREY

Some of these verses have appeared in the following magazines and are reprinted through the courtesy of: *American Magazine, Coronet, Cosmopolitan, Esquire, Fiction Parade, Flair, '47, '48, Glamour, Good Housekeeping, Harper's Bazaar, Harper's Magazine, House & Garden, Ladies' Home Journal, Life, Look, McCall's Magazine, Mademoiselle, Magazine of Fantasy and Science Fiction, Man's Magazine, Nash's, New York Herald Tribune TV and Radio Magazine, New Yorker, Promenade, Saturday Evening Post, Saturday Review of Literature, Sport, This Week, Titbits, True, the Man's Magazine, Vogue, What's New* (Abbott Laboratories), *Woman's Day.*

# CONTENTS

---

[ xi ]

THE PRIVATE DINING ROOM

MANY LONG YEARS AGO

I'M A STRANGER HERE MYSELF

GOOD INTENTIONS

[ xvi ]

# INTRODUCTION

There seem to be at least three Ogden Nashes. There are, for example: (1) the experimental craftsman, (2) the social critic and (3) the skylarking humorist. Sometimes Nash keeps these three selves fairly well segregated. But, more often than not, he lets down the bars and allows (1) the innovator, (2) the philosopher and (3) the funny fellow to kick up their heels in happy unison. This volume is chiefly given over to the best of those tripartite romps.

It was Nash in his role of experimental craftsman who first made readers aware that something new had happened to light verse in America. Accustomed to smoothly paired rhymes and neatly measured stanzas, readers were suddenly stopped by the impact of lines like:

I sit in an office at 244 Madison Avenue
And say to myself you have a responsible job, havenue?

Cajoled by talk of babies, even parents were startled to find:

A bit of talcum
Is always walcum.

The reader of Nash learned his lessons in a new school; he learned of too much affection which:

. . . leads to breaches of promise
If you go lavishing it around on red hot momise.

He pondered the theatrical reflection that:

In the Vanities
No one wears panities.

He learned to decipher the weird but comforting axiom that:

A girl who is bespectacled,
She may not get her necktacled;
But safety pins and bassinets
Await the girl who fassinets.

Here and elsewhere Nash invents lines that run blithely on without benefit of meter and rhymes so madcap as to be irresponsible. Instead of pleasing the reader with the customary niceties, Nash assaults him with a series of breathless outrages. One or two fanatical source-hunters claim to have found the origin of Nash's eccentric lines in W. S. Gilbert's "Lost Mr. Blake." But an unprejudiced comparison will show that the two styles have little in common and that, whereas Gilbert made the experiment just once, Nash uses it so freely and so efficiently that he has put his trademark upon it.

So with the rhymes. Nash is the master of surprising words that nearly-but-do-not-quite match, words which rhyme reluctantly, words which never before had any relation with each other and which will never be on rhyming terms again. Here are those apparently improvised monologues in which the distortions are more lively—and more quotable—than any prepared accuracy.

What would you do if you were up a dark alley with Caesar
   Borgia
And he was coming torgia . . .

But the slightly lunatic manner is deceptive. Disguised as the buffoon who cannot resist a parody and a pun—"only God can make a trio"—there is the social critic. Here again Nash has a fresh set of surprises up his ample sleeve. Just as the reader has concluded that all Nash's lampoons are as light and amiable as, say, "Oh, Please Don't Get Up!" the poet uses a swift and two-edged sword to express—and expose—the mocking courtesy of "The Japanese." Accomplishing its devastation in eight short lines, "The Japanese" should convince the reader that, contrary to what he may have been led to expect, Nash's finest effects are not in the madly tortuous lines and bewildered rhymes, but in the straightforward couplets and quatrains. Even without his unique bag of technical tricks, Nash creates the deftest light verse being written today. The longer and more elaborately contrived poems are topical and timely; but there is something dateless in the nimble gallantry of "To a Lady Passing Time Better Left Unpassed," the whimsical appeal of "Complaint to Four Angels," the submerged but not too suppressed anger of "To a Small Boy Standing on My Shoes While I Am Wearing Them," the affable sentiment of "An Introduction to Dogs," and the merry malice in what is perhaps the most philosophic and certainly the funniest poem in the collection, "The Seven Spiritual Ages of Mrs. Marmaduke Moore."

Nash the rhyming clown may win us first, but it is Nash the laughing philosopher who holds us longest. Only Nash could have combined the tones of banter and burlesque to tell us:

> Our daily diet grows odder and odder—
> It's a wise child that knows its fodder.

Finally, there emerges from this collection a portrait of Nash himself, the whole person not quite concealed by the poet. We are made aware of his intimate dislikes or (since most of them begin with a "p") his prejudices; they include politicians and people's names and parsley ("parsley is gharsely") and poems by Edgar A. Guest and professors and parties next door. We see him leaping without effort from childlike fancy to mature irony; a crazy storyteller one moment, a satirist the next, a wry clown and a chuckling critic. It is then that we recognize how rounded the man really is, how much more than the haphazard rhymer he reveals. His is an inspired method which has just the right measure of madness in it, a recklessness that is never without reason. In other and flatter words, Nash is our greatest combiner of common sense and uncommon nonsense, the undisputed American heir of Edward Lear, Lewis Carroll and W. S. Gilbert.

LOUIS UNTERMEYER

[ xxi ]

VERSUS

## THE HUNTER

The hunter crouches in his blind
'Neath camouflage of every kind,
And conjures up a quacking noise
To lend allure to his decoys.
This grown-up man, with pluck and luck
Is hoping to outwit a duck.

---

## A WORD ABOUT WINTER

Now the frost is on the pane,
Rugs upon the floor again,
Now the screens are in the cellar,
Now the student cons the speller,
Lengthy summer noon is gone,
Twilight treads the heels of dawn,
Round-eyed sun is now a squinter,
Tiptoe breeze a panting sprinter,
Every cloud a blizzard hinter,
Squirrel on the snow a printer,
Rain spout sprouteth icy splinter,
Willy-nilly, this is winter.

Summer-swollen doorjambs settle,
Ponds and puddles turn to metal,
Skater whoops in frisky fettle,
Golf-club stingeth like a nettle,
Radiator sings like kettle,
Hearth is Popocatepetl.

Runneth nose and chappeth lip,
Draft evadeth weather strip,
Doctor wrestleth with grippe
In never-ending rivalship.

[ 3 ]

Rosebush droops in garden shoddy,
Blood is cold and thin in body,
Weary postman dreams of toddy,
Head before the heart grows noddy.

On the hearth the embers gleam,
Glowing like a maiden's dream,
Now the apple and the oak
Paint the sky with chimney smoke,
Husband now, without disgrace,
Dumps ash trays in the fireplace.

---

## HOW DO YOU SAY HA–HA IN FRENCH?

There are several people who I can claim I am glad I am not,
      without being accused of pride and effrontery,
And one of them is the bartender of a French restaurant in an
      English-speaking country.
The conversation of the customers isn't calculated to keep a
      bartender young,
Even when they converse in their mother tongue;
How much more dispiriting it must be when after the second
      Martini
They request a third because the first two are, not finished,
      but *finis*.
They select a *Maryland*, or cigarette,
And instead of Gotta light? it is *Avez-vous une allumette?*
When they cry *Garçon* after the school of Stratford atte
      Bowe or New Rochelle or Nineveh,
It is moot whether they want the waiter or Mrs. Miniver.
Somehow, in a *bistro*, or French eatery,
Everybody suddenly discovers they can talk like Sasha Guitry,
But they really can't,
And if I were the bartender I should poke them in the *œil*
      with the *plume de ma tante*.

# WHAT I KNOW ABOUT LIFE

I have recently been pondering the life expectancy which the
    Bible allots to man,
And at this point I figure I have worked my way through
    nine-fourteenths of my hypothetical span.
I have been around a bit and met many interesting people
    and made and lost some money and acquired in reverse
    order a family and a wife,
And by now I should have drawn some valuable conclusions
    about life.
Well I have learned that life is something about which you
    can't conclude anything except that it is full of vicissi-
    tudes.
And when you expect logic you only come across eccentric-
    itudes,
Life has a tendency to obfuscate and bewilder,
Such as fating us to spend the first part of our lives being em-
    barrassed by our parents and the last part being embar-
    rassed by our childer.
Life is constantly presenting us with experiences which are
    unprecedented and depleting,
Such as the friend who starts drinking at three in the after-
    noon and explains it's only to develop a hearty appetite
    for dinner because it's unhealthy to drink without eating.
Life being what it is I don't see why everybody doesn't de-
    velop an ulcer,
Particularly Mrs. Martingale, the wife of a prominent pastry
    cook from Tulsa.
He had risen to fame and fortune after starting as a humble
    purveyor of noodles,
So he asked her what she wanted for her birthday and she
    said a new Studebaker and he thought she said a new
    strudel baker and she hated strudels.
So all I know about life is that it has been well said
That such things can't happen to a person when they are
    dead.

## FIRST LIMICK

An old person of Troy
Is so prudish and coy
That it doesn't know yet
If it's a girl or a boy.

———————

## THE STRANGE CASE OF MR. PALLISER'S PALATE

Once there was a man named Mr. Palliser and he asked his
    wife, May I be a *gourmet?*
And she said, You sure may,
But she also said, If my kitchen is going to produce a Cordon
    Blue,
It won't be me, it will be you,
And he said, You mean *Cordon Bleu?*
And she said to never mind the pronunciation so long as it
    was him and not *heu.*
But he wasn't discouraged; he bought a white hat and *The
    Cordon Bleu Cook Book* and said, How about some
    *Huîtres en Robe de Chambre?*
And she sniffed and said, Are you reading a cookbook or For-
    ever *Ambre?*
And he said, Well, if you prefer something more Anglo-Saxon,
Why suppose I whip up some tasty *Filets de Sole Jackson,*
And she pretended not to hear, so he raised his voice and
    said, Could I please you with some *Paupiettes de Veau à
    la Grecque* or *Cornets de Jambon Lucullus* or perhaps
    some nice *Moules à la Bordelaise?*
And she said, Kindly lower your voice or the neighbors will
    think we are drunk and *disordelaise,*
And she said, Furthermore the whole idea of your cooking
    anything fit to eat is a farce. So what did Mr. Palliser
    do then?
Well, he offered her *Œufs Farcis Maison* and *Homard Farci*

[6]

St. *Jacques* and *Tomate Farcie à la Bayonne* and *Auber-gines Farcies Provençales,* as well as *Aubergines Farcies Italiennes,*

And she said, Edward, kindly accompany me as usual to Ham-burger Heaven and stop playing the fool,

And he looked in the book for one last suggestion and it sug-gested *Croques Madame,* so he did, and now he dines every evening on *Crème de Concombres Glacée, Côte-lettes de Volaille Vicomtesse,* and *Artichauds à la Bari-goule.*

---

## WILL YOU HAVE YOUR TEDIUM
## RARE OR MEDIUM?

Two things I have never understood: first, the difference be-tween a Czar and a Tsar,

And second, why some people who should be bores aren't, and others, who shouldn't be, are.

I know a man who isn't sure whether bridge is played with a puck or a ball,

And he hasn't read a book since he bogged down on a poly-syllable in the second chapter of *The Rover Boys at Put-nam Hall.*

His most thrilling exploit was when he recovered a souvenir of the World's Fair that had been sent out with the trash,

And the only opinion he has ever formed by himself is that he looks better without a mustache.

Intellectually speaking, he has neither ears to hear with nor eyes to see with,

Yet he is pleasing to be with.

I know another man who is an expert on everything from witchcraft and demonology to the Elizabethan drama,

And he has spent a week end with the Dalai Lama,

And substituted for a mongoose in a fight with a cobra, and performed a successful underwater appendectomy,

[7]

And I cannot tell you how tediously his reminiscences affect
 me.
I myself am fortunate in that I have many interesting thoughts
 which I express in terms that make them come alive,
And I certainly would entertain my friends if they always
 didn't have to leave just when I arrive.

---

## THE PORCUPINE

Any hound a porcupine nudges
Can't be blamed for harboring grudges.
I know one hound that laughed all winter
At a porcupine that sat on a splinter.

---

## THERE'S NOTHING LIKE INSTINCT.
## FORTUNATELY.

I suppose that plumbers' children know more about plumbing
 than plumbers do, and welders' children more about
 welding than welders,
Because the only fact in an implausible world is that all young
 know better than their elders.
A young person is a person with nothing to learn,
One who already knows that ice does not chill and fire does
 not burn.
It knows that it can read indefinitely in the dark and do its
 eyes no harm,
It knows it can climb on the back of a thin chair to look for
 a sweater it left on the bus without falling and breaking
 an arm.

[ 8 ]

It knows it can spend six hours in the sun on its first day at
    the beach without ending up a skinless beet,
And it knows it can walk barefoot through the barn without
    running a nail in its feet.
It knows it doesn't need a raincoat if it's raining or galoshes
    if it's snowing,
And knows how to manage a boat without ever having done
    any sailing or rowing.
It knows after every sporting contest that it had really picked
    the winner,
And that its appetite is not affected by eating three chocolate
    bars covered with peanut butter and guava jelly, fifteen
    minutes before dinner.
Most of all it knows
That only other people catch colds through sitting around in
    drafts in wet clothes.
Meanwhile psychologists grow rich
Writing that the young are ones parents should not under-
    mine the self-confidence of which.

---

## THE PEOPLE UPSTAIRS

The people upstairs all practice ballet.
Their living room is a bowling alley.
Their bedroom is full of conducted tours.
Their radio is louder than yours.
They celebrate week ends all the week.
When they take a shower, your ceilings leak.
They try to get their parties to mix
By supplying their guests with Pogo sticks,
And when their orgy at last abates,
They go to the bathroom on roller skates.
I might love the people upstairs wondrous
If instead of above us, they just lived under us.

[ 9 ]

## TABLEAU AT TWILIGHT

I sit in the dusk. I am all alone.
Enter a child and an ice-cream cone.

A parent is easily beguiled
By sight of this coniferous child.

The friendly embers warmer gleam,
The cone begins to drip ice cream.

Cones are composed of many a vitamin.
My lap is not the place to bitamin.

Although my raiment is not chinchilla,
I flinch to see it become vanilla.

Coniferous child, when vanilla melts
I'd rather it melted somewhere else.

Exit child with remains of cone.
I sit in the dusk. I am all alone,

Muttering spells like an angry Druid,
Alone, in the dusk, with the cleaning fluid.

---

## THERE ARE MORE WAYS TO ROAST A PIG
## THAN BURNING THE HOUSE DOWN
### or
## YOU CAN ALWAYS STICK YOUR HEAD
## IN A VOLCANO

Poring over calendars is apt to give people round shoulders
and a squint, or strabismus,

So I am perhaps fortunate in not needing a calendar to tell
me when it's my birthday or Christmas.
I know that a year has rolled around once more
When I find myself thumbing a crisp new cigarette lighter
just like the coven of other cigarette lighters strewn on
a shelf in the garage along with the broken tire chains
and the license plates for 1934.
It is only for myself that I presume to speak,
But I can light cigarettes with a cigarette lighter for exactly
one week,
And then on the eighth day something comes up for renewal,
And sometimes it's the flint, and maybe the powder horn or
ramrod, and sometimes the fuel,
And if it's the flint you unscrew the little jigger at the bottom
and the insides jump out at you like a jack-in-the-box
and you can't get them back in without the services of
an engineer and a gunsmith and a vet,
And if it's the fuel it gets everywhere except into the tank
and when you spin the wheel the whole thing including
your hand flares up like a crêpe Suzette.
Well, enough is enough,
And many less ingenious persons would turn to chewing cut
plug, or sniffing snuff,
But in between birthdays and Christmases I have figured out
a way to light cigarettes indoors and out in any kind of
weather;
I just rub a match and a matchbox together.

---

SEPTEMBER IS SUMMER, TOO
or
IT'S NEVER TOO LATE TO BE UNCOMFORTABLE

Well, well, well, so this is summer, isn't that *mirabile dictu,*
And these are the days when whatever you sit down on you
stick to.

These are the days when those who sell four ounces of synthetic lemonade concocted in a theater basement for a quarter enter into their inheritance,

And Rum Collinses soak through paper napkins onto people's Hepplewhites and Sheratons,

And progressive-minded citizens don their most porous finery and frippery.

But it doesn't help, because underneath they are simultaneously sticky and slippery.

And some insomniacs woo insomnia plus pajamas and others minus,

And everybody patronizes air-conditioned shops and movies to get cool and then complains that the difference in temperature gives them lumbago and sinus,

And people trapped in doorways by thunderstorms console themselves by saying, Well, anyway this will cool it off while we wait,

So during the storm the mercury plunges from ninety-four to ninety-three and afterwards climbs immediately to ninety-eight,

And marriages break up over such momentous questions as Who ran against Harding—Davis or Cox?

And when you go to strike a match the head dissolves on the box,

But these estival phenomena amaze me not,

What does amaze me is how every year people are amazed to discover that summer is hot.

---

## THE LION

Oh, weep for Mr. and Mrs. Bryan!
He was eaten by a lion;
Following which, the lion's lioness
Up and swallowed Bryan's Bryaness.

## THIRD LIMICK

Two nudists of Dover,
Being purple all over,
Were munched by a cow
When mistaken for clover.

---

## POSSESSIONS ARE NINE POINTS OF CONVERSATION

Some people, and it doesn't matter whether they are paupers
    or millionaires,
Think that anything they have is the best in the world just
    because it is theirs.
If they happen to own a 1921 jalopy,
They look at their neighbor's new de luxe convertible like the
    wearer of a 57th Street gown at a 14th Street copy.
If their seventeen-year-old child is still in the third grade they
    sneer at the graduation of the seventeen-year-old chil-
    dren of their friends,
Claiming that prodigies always come to bad ends,
And if their roof leaks,
It's because the shingles are antiques.
Other people, and it doesn't matter if they are Scandinavians
    or Celts,
Think that anything is better than theirs just because it be-
    longs to somebody else.
If you congratulate them when their blue-blooded Doberman
    pinscher wins the obedience championship, they look
    at you like a martyr,
And say that the garbage man's little Rover is really infinitely
    smarter;
And if they smoke fifteen-cent cigars they are sure somebody
    else gets better cigars for a dime.
And if they take a trip to Paris they are sure their friends who
    went to Old Orchard had a better time.

[ 13 ]

Yes, they look on their neighbor's ox and ass with covetousness and their own ox and ass with abhorrence,

And if they are wives they want their husbands to be like Florence's Freddie, and if they are husbands they want their wives to be like Freddie's Florence.

I think that comparisons are truly odious, I do not approve of this constant proud or envious to-do;

And furthermore, dear friends, I think that you and yours are delightful and I also think that me and mine are delightful too.

---

## POLTERGUEST, MY POLTERGUEST

I've put Miss Hopper upon the train,
And I hope to do so never again,
For must I do so, I shouldn't wonder
If, instead of upon it, I put her under.

Never has host encountered a visitor
Less desirabler, less exquisiter,
Or experienced such a tangy zest
In beholding the back of a parting guest.

Hoitiful-toitiful Hecate Hopper
Haunted our house and haunted it proper,
Hecate Hopper left the property
Irredeemably Hecate Hopperty.

The morning paper was her monopoly
She read it first, and Hecate Hopperly,
Handing on to the old subscriber
A wad of Dorothy Dix and fiber.

Shall we coin a phrase for "to unco-operate"?
How about trying "to Hecate Hopperate"?

[ 14 ]

On the maid's days off she found it fun
To breakfast in bed at quarter to one.

Not only was Hecate on a diet,
She insisted that all the family try it,
And all one week end we gobbled like pigs
On rutabagas and salted figs.

She clogged the pipes and she blew the fuses,
She broke the rocker that Grandma uses,
And she ran amok in the medicine chest,
Hecate Hopper, the Polterguest.

Hecate Hopper the Polterguest
Left stuff to be posted or expressed,
And absconded, her suavity undiminished,
With a mystery story I hadn't finished.

If I pushed Miss Hopper under the train
I'd probably have to do it again,
For the time that I pushed her off the boat
I regretfully found Miss Hopper could float.

---

## PIANO TUNER, UNTUNE ME THAT TUNE

I regret that before people can be reformed they have to be
    sinners,
And that before you have pianists in the family you have to
    have beginners.
When it comes to beginners' music
I am not enthusic.
When listening to something called "An Evening in My Doll
    House," or "Buzz Buzz, Said the Bee to the Clover,"
Why I'd like just once to hear it played all the way through,
    instead of that hard part near the end over and over.
Have you noticed about little fingers?

[ 15 ]

When they hit a sour note, they lingers.
And another thing about little fingers, they are always straw-
berry-jammed or cranberry-jellied-y,
And "Chopsticks" is their favorite melody,
And if there is one man who I hope his dentist was a sadist
and all his teeth were brittle ones,
It is he who invented "Chopsticks" for the little ones.
My good wishes are less than frugal
For him who started the little ones going boogie-woogal,
But for him who started the little ones picking out "Chop-
sticks" on the ivories,
Well I wish him a thousand harems of a thousand wives
apiece, and a thousand little ones by each wife, and each
little one playing "Chopsticks" twenty-four hours a day
in all the nurseries of all his harems, or wiveries.

PAPPY WANTS A POPPY

When I a winsome babe did creep,
I'm told that I was fond of sleep,
And later, as a handsome stripling,
Gave up my life to sleep and Kipling.
At thirty, proud and in my prime,
They found me sleeping half the time,
And now that I am forty-four,
Why, sleep I doubly do adore.
As headlines range from odd to oddest
My own requirements grow more modest;
I ask no cloud of daffodils,
But just a cask of sleeping pills.
Wrapped in a robe of rosy slumber
How happily my dreams I number:
Europe erupts in bumper crops;
Bubble Gum King swells up and pops;
Big hussy novel wilts on cob;
In Georgia, Negro lynches mob;

The Have-nots simply love the Haves,
And people understand the Slavs;
Good fairies pay my income taxes,
And Mrs. Macy shops at Saks's.
In an era opened by mistake
I'd rather sleep than be awake.
Indeed, at times I can't recall
Why ever I wake up at all.

---

## NOT EVEN FOR BRUNCH

When branches bend in fruitful stupor
Before the woods break out in plaid,
The super-market talks more super,
The roadside stands go slightly mad.
What garden grew this goblin harvest?
Who coined these words that strike me numb?
I will not purchase, though I starvest,
The cuke, the glad, the lope, the mum.

In happier days I sank to slumber
Murmuring names as sweet as hope:
Fair gladiolus, and cucumber,
Chrysanthemum and cantaloupe.
I greet the changelings that awoke me
With warmth a little less than luke,
As farmer and florist crowd to choke me
With glad and lope, with mum and cuke.

Go hence, far hence, you jargon-mongers,
Go soak your head in boiling ads,
Go feed to cuttlefish and congers
Your mums and lopes, your cukes and glads.
Stew in the whimsy that you dole us;
I roam where magic casements ope

On cantemum spiced, and cuciolus,
On chrysanthecumber, and gladaloupe.

---

## MRS. PURVIS DREADS ROOM SERVICE
### or
## MR. PURVIS DREADS IT, TOO

Some say the fastest living creature is the cheetah,
Others nominate a duenna getting between a señor and a
    señorita,
Which goes to show that their knowledge of natural history
    is clear as a bell,
But they've never had their clothes off in a hotel.
Some hold out for the speed with which a Wagnerian quits
    an opera by Puccini,
Others for the speed with which an empty stomach is hit by
    a dry Martini.
These are speeds on whose superior speediness they persis-
    tently dwell,
Which simply proves that they've never had their clothes off
    in a hotel.
If you want to spite your face you can cut your nose off,
And if you want to spite people who think that cheetahs and
    duennas and dry Martinis are speedy, you can go to a
    hotel and take your clothes off,
Because some people can run the hundred in ten seconds and
    others would need only nine to circle the earth at the
    equator,
And they are the ones who knock on your triple-locked door
    just as you're ready for the bath and before you can say
    Wait a minute! they stalk in and if you're a man they're
    the maid and if you're a woman they're the waiter.
So I say Hats off to our hotel managers,
I hope they all get mistaken for Japanese beetles by scarlet
    tanagers,

Because there are two dubious thrills they guarantee every
     guest,
And one is a fleet-footed staff that laughs at locksmiths, be-
     cause the other is a triple lock that will open only from
     the outside and only if the inmate is completely un-
     dressed.

---

## OH SHUCKS, MA'AM, I MEAN EXCUSE ME

The greatest error ever erred
Is a nice girl with a naughty word.
For naughty words I hold no brief,
They fill my modest heart with grief,
But since it's plainer every day,
That naughty words are here to stay,
At least let's send them back again
To where they come from: namely, men.
For men, although to language prone,
Know when to leave the stuff alone;
The stevedore, before each damn,
Stops to consider where he am;
The lumberjack is careful, too,
Of what he says in front of who;
And if surrounded by the young,
The taxi driver curbs his tongue.
The reason men speak softly thus is
That circumstances alter cusses,
And naughty words scream out like sirens
When uttered in the wrong environs.
But maidens who restrict their hips
Place no such limits on their lips;
Once they have learned a startling Verb,
No tactful qualms their heads disturb;
They scatter Adjectives hither and thence
Regardless of their audience,

And cannot hold a Noun in trust
But have to out with it, or bust,
And that's why men creep into crannies
When girls play cribbage with their grannies,
And nervous husbands develop hives
When ministers call upon their wives,
And fathers tie themselves in knots
When damsels stoop to caress their tots,
For who knows what may not be heard
From a nice girl with a naughty word?
One truth all womankind nonplusses:
That circumstances alter cusses.

---

## ALWAYS MARRY AN APRIL GIRL

Praise the spells and bless the charms,
I found April in my arms.
April golden, April cloudy,
Gracious, cruel, tender, rowdy;
April soft in flowered languor,
April cold with sudden anger,
Ever changing, ever true—
I love April, I love you.

---

## LINES TO BE EMBROIDERED ON A BIB
### or
## THE CHILD IS FATHER OF THE MAN, BUT NOT FOR QUITE A WHILE

So Thomas Edison
Never drank his medicine;
So Blackstone and Hoyle

Refused cod-liver oil;
So Sir Thomas Malory
Never heard of a calory;
So the Earl of Lennox
Murdered Rizzio without the aid of vitamins or calisthenox;
So Socrates and Plato
Ate dessert without finishing their potato;
So spinach was too spinachy
For Leonardo da Vinaci:
Well, it's all immaterial,
So eat your nice cereal,
And if you want to name your own ration,
First go get a reputation.

---

## I DO, I WILL, I HAVE

How wise I am to have instructed the butler to instruct the
     first footman to instruct the second footman to instruct
     the doorman to order my carriage;
I am about to volunteer a definition of marriage.
Just as I know that there are two Hagens, Walter and Copen,
I know that marriage is a legal and religious alliance entered
     into by a man who can't sleep with the window shut and
     a woman who can't sleep with the window open.
Moreover just as I am unsure of the difference between flora
     and fauna and flotsam and jetsam
I am quite sure that marriage is the alliance of two people one
     of whom never remembers birthdays and the other never
     forgetsam,
And he refuses to believe there is a leak in the water pipe or
     the gas pipe and she is convinced she is about to asphyx-
     iate or drown,
And she says Quick get up and get my hairbrushes off the
     window sill, it's raining in, and he replies Oh they're all
     right, it's only raining straight down.

That is why marriage is so much more interesting than divorce,
Because it's the only known example of the happy meeting of
    the immovable object and the irresistible force.
So I hope husbands and wives will continue to debate and
    combat over everything debatable and combatable,
Because I believe a little incompatibility is the spice of life,
    particularly if he has income and she is pattable.

---

## THE GUPPY

Whales have calves,
Cats have kittens,
Bears have cubs,
Bats have bittens.
Swans have cygnets,
Seals have puppies,
But guppies just have little guppies.

---

## GOOD RIDDANCE, BUT NOW WHAT?

Come children, gather round my knee;
Something is about to be.

Tonight's December thirty-first,
Something is about to burst.

The clock is crouching, dark and small,
Like a time bomb in the hall.

Hark, it's midnight, children dear.
Duck! Here comes another year!

# I'LL TAKE THE HIGH ROAD COMMISSION

In between the route marks
And the shaving rhymes,
Black and yellow markers
Comment on the times.
All along the highway
Hear the signs discourse:

MEN
S L O W
WORKING

;

SADDLE
C R O S S I N G
HORSE

.

Cryptic crossroad preachers
Proffer good advice,

Helping wary drivers
Keep out of Paradise.

Transcontinental sermons,
Transcendental talk:

SOFT
C A U T I O N
SHOULDERS

;

CROSS
C H I L D R E N
WALK

.

Wisest of their proverbs,
Truest of their talk,
Have I found that dictum:

[ 23 ]

CROSS
# CHILDREN
WALK

.

When Adam took the highway
He left his sons a guide:

CROSS
# CHILDREN
WALK

;

CHEERFUL
# CHILDREN
RIDE

.

---

## THE ASP

Whenever I behold an asp
I can't suppress a startled gasp.
I do not charge the asp with matricide,
But what about his Cleopatricide?

---

## COUSIN EUPHEMIA KNOWS BEST
### or
## PHYSICIAN, HEAL SOMEBODY ELSE

Some people don't want to be doctors because they think
    doctors don't make a good living,
And also get called away from their bed at night and from
    their dinner on Christmas and Thanksgiving,

And other people don't want to be doctors because a doctor's
   friends never take their symptoms to his office at ten
   dollars a throw but insert them into a friendly game of
   gin rummy or backgammon,
And ask questions about their blood count just as the doctor
   is lining up an elusive putt or an elusive salmon.
These considerations do not influence me a particle;
I do not want to be a doctor simply because somewhere in
   the family of every patient is a female who has read an
   article.
You remove a youngster's tonsils and the result is a triumph
   of medical and surgical science,
He stops coughing and sniffling and gains eleven pounds and
   gets elected captain of the Junior Giants,
But his great-aunt spreads the word that you are a quack,
Because she read an article in the paper last Sunday where
   some Rumanian savant stated that tonsillectomy is a thing
   of the past and the Balkan hospitals are bulging with
   people standing in line to have their tonsils put back.
You suggest calamine lotion for the baby's prickly heat,
And you are at once relegated to the back seat,
Because its grandmother's cousin has seen an article in the
   "Household Hints" department of *Winning Parcheesi*
   that says the only remedy for prickly heat is homoge-
   nized streptomycin,
And somebody's sister-in-law has seen an article where the
   pathologist of *Better Houses and Trailers* says calamine
   lotion is out, a conscientious medicine man wouldn't apply calamine lotion to an itching bison.
I once read an unwritten article by a doctor saying there is
   only one cure for a patient's female relative who has
   read an article:
A hatpin in the left ventricle of the hearticle.

# HERE USUALLY COMES THE BRIDE

June means weddings in everyone's lexicon,
Weddings in Swedish, weddings in Mexican.
Breezes play Mendelssohn, treeses play Youmans,
Birds wed birds, and humans wed humans.
All year long the gentlemen woo,
But the ladies dream of a June "I do."
Ladies grow loony, and gentlemen loonier;
This year's June is next year's Junior.

---

# COMPLIMENTS OF A FRIEND

How many gifted pens have penned
That Mother is a boy's best friend!
How many more with like afflatus
Award the dog that honored status!
I hope my tongue in prune juice smothers
If I belittle dogs or mothers,
But gracious, how can I agree?
I know my own best friend is Me.
We share our joys and our aversions,
We're thicker than the Medes and Persians,
We blend like voices in a chorus,
The same things please, the same things bore us.
If I am broke, then Me needs money;
I make a joke, Me finds it funny.
I know what I like, Me knows what art is;
We hate the people at cocktail parties,
When I can stand the crowd no more,
Why, Me is halfway to the door.
I am a dodo; Me, an auk;
We grieve that pictures learned to talk;
For every sin that I produce
Kind Me can find some soft excuse,
And when I blow a final gasket,

Who but Me will share my casket?
Beside us, Pythias and Damon
We're just two unacquainted laymen.
Sneer not, for if you answer true,
Don't you feel that way about You?

---

## THE MIDDLE

When I remember bygone days
I think how evening follows morn;
So many I loved were not yet dead,
So many I love were not yet born.

---

## FOR A GOOD DOG

My little dog ten years ago
Was arrogant and spry,
Her backbone was a bended bow
For arrows in her eye.
Her step was proud, her bark was loud,
Her nose was in the sky,
But she was ten years younger then,
And so, by God, was I.

Small birds on stilts along the beach
Rose up with piping cry,
And as they flashed beyond her reach
I thought to see her fly.
If natural law refused her wings,
That law she would defy,

For she could do unheard-of things,
And so, at times, could I.

Ten years ago she split the air
To seize what she could spy;
Tonight she bumps against a chair,
Betrayed by milky eye.
She seems to pant, Time up, time up!
My little dog must die,
And lie in dust with Hector's pup;
So, presently, must I.

———————————

## THE PERFECT HUSBAND

He tells you when you've got on too much lipstick,
And helps you with your girdle when your hips stick.

# THE PRIVATE DINING ROOM

# THE PRIVATE DINING ROOM

Miss Rafferty wore taffeta,
Miss Cavendish wore lavender.
We ate pickerel and mackerel
And other lavish provender.
Miss Cavendish was Lalage,
Miss Rafferty was Barbara.
We gobbled pickled mackerel
And broke the candelabara,
Miss Cavendish in lavender,
In taffeta, Miss Rafferty,
The girls in taffeta lavender,
And we, of course, in mufti.

Miss Rafferty wore taffeta,
The taffeta was lavender,
Was lavend, lavender, lavenderest,
As the wine improved the provender.
Miss Cavendish wore lavender,
The lavender was taffeta.
We boggled mackled pickerel,
And bumpers did we quaffeta.
And Lalage wore lavender,
And lavender wore Barbara,
Rafferta taffeta Cavender lavender
Barbara abracadabra.

Miss Rafferty in taffeta
Grew definitely raffisher.
Miss Cavendish in lavender
Grew less and less stand-offisher.
With Lalage and Barbara
We grew a little pickereled,
We ordered Mumm and Roederer
Because the bubbles tickereled.
But lavender and taffeta
Were gone when we were soberer.

I haven't thought for thirty years
Of Lalage and Barbara.

------

## PEEKABOO, I ALMOST SEE YOU

Middle-aged life is merry, and I love to lead it,
But there comes a day when your eyes are all right but your
    arm isn't long enough to hold the telephone book where
    you can read it,
And your friends get jocular, so you go to the oculist,
And of all your friends he is the joculist,
So over his facetiousness let us skim,
Only noting that he has been waiting for you ever since you
    said Good evening to his grandfather clock under the
    impression that it was him,
And you look at his chart and it says SHRDLU QWERTYOP,
    and you say Well, why SHRDNTLU QWERTYOP? and
    he says one set of glasses won't do.
You need two,
One for reading Erle Stanley Gardner's Perry Mason and
    Keats's "Endymion" with,
And the other for walking around without saying Hello to
    strange wymion with.
So you spend your time taking off your seeing glasses to put
    on your reading glasses, and then remembering that your
    reading glasses are upstairs or in the car,
And then you can't find your seeing glasses again because
    without them on you can't see where they are.
Enough of such mishaps, they would try the patience of an
    ox,
I prefer to forget both pairs of glasses and pass my declining
    years saluting strange women and grandfather clocks.

## CORRECTION: *EVE* DELVED AND *ADAM* SPAN

The ladies of the garden club
Are in the other room,
And, fed on tea and sandwiches,
Their pretty fancies bloom,
I hear their gentle treble hubbub,
The ladies of the garden clubbub.

The ladies of the garden club,
Their words are firm and sure,
They know the lore of lime and mulch,
The poetry of manure.
Each spring they beautify our suburb,
The ladies of the garden clubburb.

Dear ladies of the garden club,
I love your natural zeal,
Your verdant thumbs, your canvas gloves,
The pads on which you kneel,
But I hear you making plans involving
Husbands in gardening instead of golfing.

Between the outer door and me
The flower ladies sit.
I'm frantic-footed, blind, and trapped,
Like mole in compost pit,
One timorous masculine minutia,
Caught between baby's-breath and fuchsia.

The air is sweet with talk of bulbs,
And phlox and mignonettes;
Arrangements drape the drawer that holds
My only cigarettes.
Would I had courage for an end run
Round herbaceous border and rhododendron!

Ranunculus can a prison make,
And hyacinth a cell;

I barely glimpse a patch of sky
Through wreath of immortelle.
And thus are fulfilled the baleful prophecies
Concerning men who are at home instead of their offices.

---

## MY TRIP DAORBA

I have just returned from a foreign tour,
But ask me not what I saw, because I am not sure.
Not being a disciplinarian like Father Day,
I saw everything the wrong way,
Because of one thing about Father Day I am sure,
Which is that he would not have ridden backwards so that
    the little Days could ride forwards on their foreign tour.
Indeed I am perhaps the only parent to be found
Who saw Europe, or eporuE, as I think of it, the wrong way
    round.
I added little to my knowledge of the countryside but much
    to my reputation for docility
Riding backwards through ecnarF and ylatI.
I am not quite certain,
But I think in siraP I saw the ervuoL, the rewoT leffiE, and
    the Cathedral of emaD ertoN.
I shall remember ecnerolF forever,
For that is where I backed past the house where etnaD wrote
    the "onrefnI," or ydemoC eniviD, and twisted my neck
    admiring the bridges across the onrA reviR.
In emoR I glimpsed the muroF and the nacitaV as in a mir-
    ror in the fog,
While in ecineV I admired the ecalaP s'egoD as beheld from
    the steerage of an alodnoG.
So I find conditions overseas a little hard to judge,
Because all I know is what I saw retreating from me as I rode
    backwards in compartments in the niart and in carriages
    sitting on the taes-pmuj.

[ 34 ]

# THE ANNIVERSARY

A marriage aged one
Is hardly begun;
A fling in the sun,
But it's hardly begun;
A green horse,
A stiff course,
And leagues to be run.

A marriage aged five
Is coming alive.
Watch it wither and thrive;
Though it's coming alive,
You must guess,
No or yes,
If it's going to survive.

A marriage aged ten
Is a hopeful Amen;
It's pray for it then,
And mutter Amen,
As the names
Of old flames
Sound again and again.

At twenty a marriage
Discovers its courage.
This year do not disparage,
It is comely in courage;
Past the teens,
And blue jeans,
It's a promising marriage.

Yet before twenty-one
It has hardly begun.
How tall in the sun,
Yet hardly begun!
But once come of age,

Pragmatically sage,
Oh, blithe to engage
Is sweet marri-age.

Tilt a twenty-first cup
To a marriage grown up,
Now sure and mature,
And securely grown up.
Raise twenty-one cheers
To the silly young years,
While I sit out the dance
With my dearest of dears.

---

## A CAUTION TO EVERYBODY

Consider the auk;
Becoming extinct because he forgot how to fly, and could
    only walk.
Consider man, who may well become extinct
Because he forgot how to walk and learned how to fly before
    he thinked.

---

## I DIDN'T SAY A WORD
### or
## WHO CALLED THAT PICCOLO PLAYER
## A FATHER?

A man could be granted to live a dozen lives,
And he still wouldn't understand daughters and wives.
It may be because sometimes their ears are pierced for ear-
    rings,

But they have the most eccentric hearings.
Their hearings are in fact so sensitive
That you frequently feel reprehensive.
At home, for instance, when near you,
Nobody can hear you.
After your most brilliant fireside or breakfast-table chats you
    can count on two fingers the responses you will have got:
Either, Don't mumble, dear, or, more simply, What?
I suppose if you're male and parental
You get used to being treated mental,
But you'd feel less psychically distant
If they weren't so inconsistent,
Because if you open your mouth in a hotel or a restaurant
    their eardrums quiver at every decibel,
And their embarrassment is almost, if not quite, inexprecibel.
Their eyes signal What's cooking? at you,
And their lips hiss, Shush, Daddy, everybody's looking at you!
Now, I realize that old age is a thing of beauty,
Because I have read Cicero's *De Senectute,*
But I prefer to approach senility in my own way, so I'll thank
    nobody to rush me,
By which I mean specifically that my voice in a tearoom is no
    louder than anybody else's, so why does everybody have
    to shush me?

---

## CALLING SPRING VII—MMMC

As an old traveler, I am indebted to paper-bound thrillers,
Because you travel faster from Cleveland to Terre Haute
    when you travel with a lapful of victims and killers.
I am by now an authority on thumbprints and fingerprints
    and even kneeprints.
But there is one mystery I have never been able to solve in
    certain of my invaluable reprints.

I am happily agog over their funerals, which are always satis-
    factorily followed by exhumerals,
But I can't understand why so many of them carry their copy-
    right lines in Roman numerals.
I am just as learned as can be,
But if I want to find out when a book was first published, I
    have to move my lips and count on my fingers to trans-
    late Copyright MCMXXXIII into Copyright 1933.
I have a horrid suspicion
That something lies behind the publisher's display of eru-
    dition.
I may be oversensitive to clues,
But I detect a desire to obfuscate and confuse.
Do they think that because a customer cannot translate
    MCMXXXIII into 1933 because he is not a classical
    scholar,
He will therefore assume the book to have been first pub-
    lished yesterday and will therefore sooner lay down his
    XXV cents or I/IV of a dollar?
Or do they, straying equally far from the straight and narrow,
Think that the scholarly will snatch it because the Roman
    copyright line misleads him to believe it the work of
    Q. Horatius Flaccus or P. Virgilius Maro?
Because anybody can make a mistake when dealing with
    MCMs and XLVs and things, even Jupiter, ruler of gods
    and men;
All the time he was going around with IO he pronounced
    it Ten.


EVERYBODY'S MIND TO ME A KINGDOM IS
or
A GREAT BIG WONDERFUL WORLD IT'S

Some melodies are popular as well as classical, which I sup-
    pose makes them popsicles,

And some poems are part William Cullen Bryant and part
    Nick Kenny which makes them thanatopsicles,
And to some people Wisconsin is what Guinevere was to
    Launcelot,
And if they are away from it they are Wisconsolate.
Some naturalists know why the sphinx is sphinxlike and the
    griffin is griffiny,
And some couples are so wealthy that even their tiffs are
    from Tiffany.
Some Angeleno socialites fine each other a dollar
If they say La Jolla,
And give each other a Picasso or a Goya
For pronouncing it La Hoya.
Why should not I pick up a masterpiece or a coin?
I will no longer say Des Moines,
I shall sail into the C. B. & Q. ticket office like a swan,
And ask for a lower to Day Mwahn.
This I shall do because I am a conscientious man, when I
    throw rocks at sea birds I leave no tern unstoned,
I am a meticulous man, and when I portray baboons I leave
    no stern untoned,
I am a man who values the fitness of things above notoriety
    and pelf,
Which is why I am happy I heard the cockney postmaster
    say to a doctor who was returning a leprechaun to
    Glocca Morra in an open envelope, Physician, seal thy
    h'elf.

---

## THEY WON'T BELIEVE ON NEW YEAR'S EVE, THAT NEW YEAR'S DAY WILL COME WHAT MAY

How do I feel today? I feel as unfit as an unfiddle,
And it is the result of a certain turbulence in the mind and
    an uncertain burbulence in the middle.
What was it anyway, that angry thing that flew at me?

I am unused to banshees crying Boo at me.
Your wife can't be a banshee,
Or can she?
Of course, some wives become less fond
When you're bottled in bond.
My Uncle George, in lavender-scented Aunt Edna's day,
If he had a glass of beer on Saturday night, he didn't dare come home till the following Wednesday.
I see now that he had hit upon the ideal idea,
The passage of time, and plenty of it, is the only marital panacea.
Ah, if the passage of time were backward, and last night I'd been a child again, this morning I'd be fragrant with orange juice,
Instead of reeking of pinch-bottle foreign juice;
But if I should turn out to be a child again, what would life hold for me?
The woman I love would be too old for me.
There's only one solution to my problem, a hair of the dog, or maybe a couple of hairs;
Then if she doesn't get mad at me my life will be peaceful, and if she does, it will show she really cares.

---

## DON'T LOOK FOR THE SILVER LINING, JUST WAIT FOR IT

The rabbit loves his hoppity and the wallaby loves his hip-pity.
I love my serendipity.
Let none look askance;
Serendipity is merely the knack of making happy and unexpected discoveries by chance.
Only yesterday I was bored by a bore—there is no topic that he isn't inept on it—
And when I pointed out a piece of chewing gum on the side-

walk, he was too busy talking to listen, so I soon made
the happy and unexpected discovery that he had stepped
on it.

It was serendipity when a recent hostess of mine in Philadel-
phia apologized for serving ham and eggs because she
had forgotten to order scrapple,

Just as it was when I found a bow tie I could wear that didn't
rise and fall with my Adam's apple.

Also when I found a hole in my pocket which I had tickets
for a harp recital in, or in which I had tickets for a harp
recital, to put it properer,

So instead of the harp recital we had to see the Marx Brothers in *A Night at the Opera.*

If your coat catches on a branch just as you are about to slip
over a precipice precipitous,

That's serendipitous,

But when you happily and unexpectedly discover that you
don't have to go to the dentist or the chiropodist,

That's serendopitist.

---

## THE TORTOISE

Come crown my brows with leaves of myrtle;
I know the tortoise is a turtle.
Come carve my name in stone immortal;
I know the turtoise is a tortle;
I know to my profound despair;
I bet on one to beat a hare.
I also know I'm now a pauper
Because of its tortley turtley torpor.

## THE MULES

In the world of mules
There are no rules.

---

## THE CUCKOO

Cuckoos lead Bohemian lives,
They fail as husband and as wives,
Therefore they cynically disparage
Everybody else's marriage.

---

## THE VOLUBLE WHEEL CHAIR

When you roll along admiring the view,
And everyone drives too fast but you;
When people not only ignore your advice,
But complain that you've given it to them twice;
When you babble of putts you nearly holed,
By gad, sir,
You are getting old.

When for novels you lose your appetite
Because writers don't write what they used to write;
When by current art you are unbeguiled,
And pronounce it the work of an idiot child;
When cacophonous music leaves you cold,
By gad, sir,
You are getting old.

When you twist the sheets from night to morn
To recall when a cousin's daughter was born;
When youngsters mumble and won't speak up,
And your dog dodders, who was a pup;
When the modern girl seems a hussy bold,
By gad, sir,
You are getting old.

When you scoff at feminine fashion trends;
When strangers resemble absent friends;
When you start forgetting the neighbors' names
And remembering bygone football games;
When you only drop in at the club to scold,
By gad, sir,
You are getting old.

But when you roar at the income tax,
And the slippery bureaucratic hacks,
And the ancient political fishlike smell,
And assert that the world is going to hell,
Why you are not old at all, at all;
By gad, sir,
You are on the ball.

---

## THE CHILD IS FATHER TO THE MAN,
### BUT WITH MORE AUTHORITY

Once there were some children and they were uninterested in
    chores,
And they never picked anything up or put anything back or
    brought anything in from out-of-doors.
They didn't want to take care of anything, just to play with it,
And their parents let them get away with it.
Little did they know that Nemesis
Was on the premises.

Their regrets were at first scant

When they were left alone on their island summer home because their parents were called away by the convalescence of a wealthy aunt.

They prepared to take advantage of nobody being around,

And this is what they found,

This is how they were hoist with their own petards,

There wasn't a deck with more than fifty-one cards,

And when they tried to play the handsome phonograph with which they were equipped,

The records were either lost, warped or chipped,

There were bows but no arrows, and bats and gloves but no ball,

And the untethered rowboat had drifted beyond recall,

And when they were wet the only towels were those strewn on the bathroom floor where moisture lingers,

And when they were cold they couldn't light a fire because all the matches had been used by people seeing how far down they would burn without burning their fingers.

Such experiences certainly taught them a lesson, and when their parents returned to their native heath,

Why, the first thing these children did was to leave the window open so it rained in on the piano, and go to bed without brushing their teeth.

---

## A DOG'S BEST FRIEND IS HIS ILLITERACY

It has been well said that quietness is what a Grecian urn is the still unravished bride of,

And that a door is what a dog is perpetually on the wrong side of.

I may add that a sachet is what many a housewife's linen is fragrantly entrusted to,

But that a cliché is what a dog owner must eventually get adjusted to.

What does the visitor say when your dog greets him with
    Southern hospitality and salutes him all kissin'-cousiny?
He says, He smells my dog on me, doesn't he?
And he asks, How old is he, and you say Twelve, and he ap-
    praises Spot with the eye of an antiquarian,
And says, Seven twelves are eighty something, why Spot in
    human terms you're an octogenarian,
But these two bromides are just the rattle before the strike,
Because then he says it's funny but he's noticed how often
    dogs and their masters look alike.
Such are the comments faced by dog owners from Peoria to
    Peshawar,
And frequently from a man who in canine terms is 322 years
    old, and he is the spit and image of his own Chihuahua.
The only escape is to have something instead of dogs but
    whatever I substituted I should probably err,
And if I ended up with raccoons every guest would turn out
    to be a raccoonteur.

------

## EVERYBODY WANTS TO GET INTO
## THE BAEDEKER

Most travelers eavesdrop
As unintentionally as autumn leaves drop,
Which brings up a question that confronts every conscientious
    traveler:
Should he, or should he not, of overheard misinformation be
    an unraveler?
The dear little old lady in front of you asks, What river is
    that, is it the Swanee or the Savannah?
And somebody who has no idea firmly says, It's the Potomac.
    It happens to be the Susquehanna.
The visiting Englishman asks, What is that mountain, and
    somebody yells, Pike's Peak! into his ear.
It isn't. It's Mt. Rainier.

Can one oneself of responsibility disembarrass
When one hears a fellow passenger being assured that the
    *Île de France* sails right up the Seine to Paris?
What is the etiquette
When one hears an eager sight-seer being informed that
    Greenwich Village is in Connecticut?
It is my experience that people who volunteer information are
    people who don't know the Eiffel Tower from the Tower
    of Pisa,
Or Desdemona from the Mona Lisa.
I am convinced that they have learned their geography
    through drawing mustaches on girls on travel posters,
And have done their own traveling exclusively on roller
    coasters.
*What is that, madam? How do you get from 42nd Street and*
    *Broadway to Times Square?*
*Sorry, madam, but it's impossible to get from here to there.*

---

## THE STRANGE CASE OF THE CAUTIOUS MOTORIST

Have you read the biography of Mr. Schwellenbach? You
    can miss it if you try.
Mr. Schwellenbach didn't have much to live for, but he didn't
    want to die.
Statistics of automobile fatalities filled his brain,
And he never drove over 25 miles an hour, and always, I re-
    gret to say, in the left-hand lane.
Whenever he stopped for a red light he cut off the ignition,
    put on the hand brake, locked all the doors, checked his
    license and registration cards, and looked in the glove
    compartment to see if he had mice,
So when the light turned green everybody behind him had to
    wait while he de-moused the car, reassured himself that
    he was driving legally, unlocked the doors, released the

[ 46 ]

hand brake, reignited the ignition, pressed the wrong but-
    ton and turned on Bing Crosby instead of the motor,
    and the light turned from green to red to green thrice.
Every autumn with the rains
Mr. Schwellenbach bought a new pair of chains.
He kept a record of every lethal blowout in the Western
    Hemisphere since 1921 in his files,
And he turned in his tires for new ones every 750 miles.
Well, he was driving on his new tires at 25 miles an hour in
    the left-hand lane of a dual highway last week, was Mr.
    Schwellenbach,
And a car coming the other way owned by a loan shark who
    had bought his old tires cheap had a blowout and
    jumped the dividing line and knocked him to hellenbach.

---

## THE UNWINGED ONES

I don't travel on planes.
I travel on trains.
Once in a while, on trains,
I see people who travel on planes.
Every once in a while I'm surrounded
By people whose planes have been grounded.
I'm enthralled by their air-minded snobbery,
Their exclusive hobnobbery.
They feel that they have to explain
How they happen to be on a train,
For even in Drawing Room A
They seem to feel déclassé.
So they sit with portentous faces
Clutching their attaché cases.
They grumble and fume about how
They'd have been in Miami by now.
By the time that they're passing through Rahway
They should be in Havana or Norway,

And they strongly imply that perhaps,
Since they're late, the world will collapse.
Sometimes on the train I'm surrounded
By people whose planes have been grounded.
That's the only trouble with trains;
When it fogs, when it smogs, when it rains,
You get people from planes.

---

## MEDUSA AND THE MOT JUSTE

Once there was a Greek divinity of the sea named Ceto and
she married a man named Phorcus,
And the marriage must have been pretty raucous;
Their remarks about which child took after which parent
must have been full of asperities,
Because they were the parents of the Gorgons, and the
Graeae, and Scylla, and the dragon that guarded the
apples of the Hesperides.
Bad blood somewhere.
Today the Gorgons are our topic, and as all schoolboys in-
cluding you and me know,
They were three horrid sisters named Medusa and Euryale
and Stheno,
But what most schoolboys don't know because they never
get beyond their Silas Marners and their Hiawathas,
The Gorgons were not only monsters, they were also highly
talented authors.
Medusa began it;
She wrote *Forever Granite*.
But soon Stheno and Euryale were writing, too, and they ad-
dressed her in daily choruses,
Saying we are three literary sisters just like the Brontës so in-
stead of Gorgons why can't we be brontësauruses?
Well, Medusa may have been mythical but she wasn't mys-
tical,

[ 48 ]

She was selfish and egotistical.
She saw wider vistas
Than simply being the sister of her sisters.
She replied, tossing away a petrified Argonaut on whom she
    had chipped a molar,
You two can be what you like, but since I am the big *fro-*
    *mage* in this family, I prefer to think of myself as the
    Gorgon Zola.

---

## EVERYTHING'S HAGGIS IN HOBOKEN
### or
## SCOTS WHA HAE HAE

That hero my allegiance earns
Who boldly speaks of Robert Burns.
I have an inexpensive hobby—
Simply not to call him Bobbie.
It's really just as easy as not
Referring to Sir Wally Scott,
But many, otherwise resolute,
When mentioning Burns go coy and cute,
Scholars hip-deep in Homer and Horace
Suddenly turn all doch-an-dorris;
Fine ladies who should pose and purr
Roll out a half-rolled Highland burr;
Conventioneers in littered lobby
Hoist their glasses in praise of Bobbie;
All, all Burns-happy and Bobbie-loopy,
They dandle him like a Scotian kewpie.
I'll brush away like gnats and midges
Those who quote from Bobbies Southey and Bridges;
I will not snap my Hopalong gun
At admirers of Bobbie Stevenson
(To be Bobbied is no worse, I guess,
Than being enshrined as R.L.S.);

I'd even attempt to save from drowning
Maidens who dream of Bobbie Browning;
But of Robert Burns I'm a serious fan,
He wrote like an angel and lived like a man,
And I yearn to shatter a set of crockery
On this condescending Bobbie-sockery.
Well, I'm off, before I break the law,
To read Tommy Hardy and Bernie Shaw.

---

## THE BAT

Myself, I rather like the bat,
It's not a mouse, it's not a rat.
It has no feathers, yet has wings,
It's quite inaudible when it sings.
It zigzags through the evening air
And never lands on ladies' hair,
A fact of which men spend their lives
Attempting to convince their wives.

---

## THE CHIPMUNK

My friends all know that I am shy,
But the chipmunk is twice as shy as I.
He moves with flickering indecision
Like stripes across the television.
He's like the shadow of a cloud,
Or Emily Dickinson read aloud.

## TWEEDLEDEE AND TWEEDLEDOOM

Said the Undertaker to the Overtaker,
Thank you for the butcher and the candlestick-maker,
For the polo player and the pretzel-baker,
For the lawyer and the lover and the wife-forsaker,
Thank you for my bulging, verdant acre,
Said the Undertaker to the Overtaker.
Move in, move under, said the Overtaker.

---

## I REMEMBER YULE

I guess I am just an old fogey.
I guess I am headed for the last roundup, so come along little
     dogey.
I can remember when winter was wintery and summer was
     estival;
I can even remember when Christmas was a family festival.
I can even remember when Christmas was an occasion for
     fireside rejoicing and general good will,
And now it is just the day that it's only X shopping days
     until.
What, five times a week at 8:15 P.M., do the herald angels
     sing?
That a small deposit now will buy you an option on a genuine
     diamond ring.
What is the message we receive with Good King Wenceslaus?
That if we rush to the corner of Ninth and Main we can get
     that pink mink housecoat very inexpenceslaus.
I know what came upon the midnight clear to our backward
     parents, but what comes to us?
A choir imploring us to Come all ye faithful and steal a 1939
     convertible at psychoneurotic prices from Grinning Gus.
Christmas is a sitting duck for sponsors, it's so commercial,
And yet so noncontroversial.

Well, you reverent sponsors redolent of frankincense and
    myrrh, come smear me with bear-grease and call me an
    un-American hellion,
This is my declaration of independence and rebellion.
This year I'm going to disconnect everything electrical in the
    house and spend the Christmas season like Tiny Tim and
    Mr. Pickwick;
You make me sickwick.

---

## MAYBE YOU CAN'T TAKE IT WITH YOU, BUT LOOK WHAT HAPPENS WHEN YOU LEAVE IT BEHIND

As American towns and cities I wander through,
One landmark is constant everywhere I roam;
The house that the Banker built in nineteen-two,
Dim neon tells me is now a funeral home.

---

## LECTURER IN BOOKSTORE

Behold best-selling Mr. Furneval,
Behind a pile of books to autograph,
Like a bearded lady at a carnival
Hoping to sell her fly-specked photograph.

---

## REFLECTION ON THE VERNACULAR

In cooking *petits pois*, or lesser peas,
Some use receipts, and some use recipes.
In spite of opposition warm,

I choose to use the former form.
In fact, though you may think me gossipy,
I plan to settle near Lake Ossipee,
And when my settlement is complete,
To change its name to Lake Osseipt.

---

## THIS IS MY OWN, MY NATIVE TONGUE

Often I leave my television set to listen to my wireless,
So, often I hear the same song sung by the same singer many
    times a day, because at repeating itself the wireless is
    tireless.
There is one such song from which at sleepy time I can
    hardly bear to part,
A song in which this particular singer, who apparently has of-
    fended a nameless character in an undescribed way,
    states that he apawlogizes from the bawttom of his heart.
I am familiar with various accents—I know that in Indiana
    you stress the "r" in Carmen,
And that in Georgia if a ladybug's house is on far she sends
    for the farmen,
And I have paaked my caah in Cambridge, and elsewhere
    spoken with those who raise hawgs and worship strange
    gawds—but here I am, late in life's autumn,
Suddenly confronted with somebody's apawlogies and bawt-
    tom.
I tell you whawt,
Things were different when I was a tawddling tawt.
I may have been an indifferent schawlar,
Lawling around in my blue serge suit and doodling on my
    Eton cawllar;
In fact, I didn't even pick up much knawledge
In a year at cawllege;
I guess that of normal intelligence I had only about two
    thirds,

But, by gum, I was taught, or, by gum, was I tot, to pro-
    nounce my words.
And now they've gawt me wondering:
Was it the dawn or the don that from China cross the bay
    came up thundering?
As a tot, was I tawddling or was I toddling?
When I doodled, was I dawdling or was I dodling?
I have forgawtten oll I ever knew of English, I find my posi-
    tion as an articulate mammal bewildering and awesome.
Would God I were a tender apple blawssom.

MANY LONG YEARS AGO

# NEVERTHELESS

I am not fond of Oliver Montrose.
Oliver is a person I despise;
The purple veins that bulbify his nose,
The crimson veins that irrigate his eyes.
His wheezy breath his vinous weakness shows;
He is the slave of whisky, beer and gin.
I am not fond of Oliver Montrose;
I hate the sinner. But what a warming sin!

Bibesco Poolidge is a man of jowl;
I've never seen a dewlap, but on him;
He shines with the grease of many a basted fowl;
Ten thousand sauces round his innards swim.
The ghosts of hosts of kine about him prowl,
Lamb, pig, and game blood trickles from his chin;
I cannot look on him without a scowl;
I hate the sinner. But what a luscious sin!

I do not dote on Murgatroyd Van Rust,
So tasty to the tenderest of genders.
Practically everything that has a bust
Surveys his suave ensemble and surrenders.
The way he parts his hair I do not trust;
Let the phone ring, I loathe his knowing grin.
You cannot see his diary for the dust,
I hate the sinner. Still, if one had to sin . . .

O Mammonites and spendthrifts, draw ye nigh,
Fingernail-biters and sluggards, come on in,
Consider now how tolerant am I
Who hate the sinner, yet who love the sin.

# WHEN THE DEVIL WAS SICK COULD
## HE PROVE IT?

Few things are duller
Than feeling unspecifically off-color,
Yes, you feel like the fulfilment of a dismal prophecy,
And you don't feel either exercisey or officey,
But still you can't produce a red throat or a white tongue or
    uneasy respiration or any kind of a symptom,
And it is very embarrassing that whoever was supposed to be
    passing out the symptoms skymptom,
Because whatever is the matter with you, you can't spot it
But whatever it is, you've got it,
But the question is how to prove it,
And you suck for hours on the mercury of the thermometer
    you finally sent out for and you can't move it,
And your entire system may be pneumococci'd or strepto-
    cocci'd,
But the looks you get from your loved ones are simply
    skepticocci'd,
And Conscience glares at you in her Here comes that bad
    penny way,
Crying There's nothing the matter with you, you're just try-
    ing to get out of doing something you never wanted to
    do anyway,
So you unfinger your pulse before Conscience can jeer at you
    for a fingerer,
And you begin to believe that perhaps she is right, perhaps
    you are nothing but a hypochondriacal old malingerer,
And you take a farewell look at the thermometer,
And that's when you hurl the bometer.
Yes sir, it's as good as a tonic,
Because you've got as pretty a ninety-nine point one as you'd
    wish to see in a month of bubonic.
Some people hold out for a hundred or more before they
    collapse,
But that leaves too many gaps;
As for me,

I can get a very smug Monday, Tuesday, Wednesday, Thursday, or Friday in bed out of a tenth of a degree.

It is to this trait that I am debtor

For the happy fact that on week ends I generally feel better.

---

## OH, STOP BEING THANKFUL ALL OVER THE PLACE

In the glittering collection of paste diamonds one in particular ranks very high,

And that is the often-quoted remark of the prominent and respectable dignitary who on seeing a condemned man on his way to the scaffold crashed into a thousand anthologies by remarking, There but for the grace of God go I.

Here is a deplorable illustration

Of sloppy ratiocination;

Here is a notable feat

Of one-way thinking on a two-way street.

It must certainly have been the speaker's lucky day,

Or otherwise he would have been run over by his speech turning around and coming back the other way,

Because did he stop to work out his premise to its logical conclusion? Ah no,

He just got it off and let it go,

And now whenever people are with people they want to impress with their combined greateartedness and booklearning they cry

Oh look at that condemned man on his way to the scaffold, there but for the grace of God go I.

Which is so far so good, but they neglect to continue with the heretofore unspoken balance of the theme, which is equally true,

That there but for the grace of God goes Jimmie Durante or

the Prince of Wales or Aimee Semple McPherson or Dr.
     Wellington Koo,
Or Moses or Napoleon or Cleopatra or P. T. Barnum,
Or even William or Dustin Farnum.
So away with you, all you parrot-like repeaters of high-sound-
     ing phrases that you never stop to consider what they
     actually mean,
I wouldn't allow you to stay in any college of which I was
     the Dean.
I can never listen to you without thinking Oh my,
There but for the grace of God speak I.

---

### "MY CHILD IS PHLEGMATIC . . ."
#### —ANXIOUS PARENT

Anxious Parent, I guess you have just never been around;
I guess you just don't know who are the happiest people any-
     where to be found;
So you are worried, are you, because your child is turning out
     to be phlegmatic?
Forgive me if I seem a trifle unsympathetic.
Why do you want your child to be a flashing, coruscating
     gem?
Don't you know the only peace the world can give lies not
     in flame but in phlegm?
Don't you know that the people with souls of putty
Are the only people who are sitting prutty?
*They* never get all worked up at the drop of a pin or a
     feather or a hat,
*They* never go around saying bitterly to themselves: "Oh God,
     did I really do, did I really say that?"
*They* never boil over when they read about stool pigeons get-
     ting girls into reformatories by making treacherous ad-
     vances;
*They* never get perfectly futilely harrowed about Sacco and

[ 60 ]

Vanzetti, or Alice Adamses who don't have good times
  at dances;
*They* never blink an eyelash about colleges that are going to
  the dogs because of football overemphasis;
*They* never almost die with indignation over a lynching near
  Natchez or Memphis.
No, when they eat they digest their food, and when they go
  to bed they get right to sleep,
And four phlegmatic angels a stolid watch over them keep.
Oh to be phlegmatic, Oh to be stolid, Oh to be torpid, Oh to
  be calm!
For it is only thus, Anxious Parent, that we can get through
  life without a qualm.

---

## THE PARTY

Come Arabella, fetch the cake,
On a dish with silver handles.
Oh mercy! Feel the table shake!
Lucinda, light the candles.
For Mr. Migg is thir-ty,
Is thir—ty,
Is thir——ty.
The years are crawling over him
Like wee red ants.
Oh, three times ten is thir-ty,
Is for—ty,
Is fif——ty.
The further off from England
The nearer is to France.

The little flames they bob and jig,
The dining hall is breezy.
Quick! puff your candles, Mr. Migg,
The little flames die easy.

For Mr. Migg is for-ty,
Is for—ty,
Is for——ty.
The years are crawling over him
Like wee red ants.
Oh four times ten is for-ty,
Is fif—ty,
Is six——ty,
And creeping through the icing,
The other years advance.

Why, Arabella, here's a ring!
Lucinda, here a thimble!
For Mr. Migg there's not a thing—
'Tis not, I trust, a symbol!

For Mr. Migg is fif-ty,
Is fif—ty,
Is fif——ty.
The years are crawling over him
Like wee red ants.
Oh, five times ten is fif-ty,
Is six—ty,
Is seven——ty.
Lucinda, put the cake away.
We're going to the dance.

---

## KINDLY UNHITCH THAT STAR, BUDDY

I hardly suppose I know anybody who wouldn't rather be a
success than a failure,
Just as I suppose every piece of crabgrass in the garden would
much rather be an azalea,
And in celestial circles all the run-of-the-mill angels would
rather be archangels or at least cherubim and seraphim,

[ 62 ]

And in the legal world all the little process-servers hope to
    grow up into great big bailiffim and sheriffim.
Indeed, everybody wants to be a wow,
But not everybody knows exactly how.
Some people think they will eventually wear diamonds in-
    stead of rhinestones
Only by everlastingly keeping their noses to their ghrinestones,
And other people think they will be able to put in more time
    at Palm Beach and the Ritz
By not paying too much attention to attendance at the office
    but rather in being brilliant by starts and fits.
Some people after a full day's work sit up all night getting a
    college education by correspondence,
While others seem to think they'll get just as far by devoting
    their evenings to the study of the difference in tempera-
    ment between brunettance and blondance.
In short, the world is filled with people trying to achieve suc-
    cess,
And half of them think they'll get it by saying No and half of
    them by saying Yes,
And if all the ones who say No said Yes, and vice versa, such
    is the fate of humanity that ninety-nine per cent of them
    still wouldn't be any better off than they were before,
Which perhaps is just as well because if everybody was a
    success nobody could be contemptuous of anybody else
    and everybody would start in all over again trying to be
    a bigger success than everybody else so they would have
    somebody to be contemptuous of and so on forevermore,
Because when people start hitching their wagons to a star,
That's the way they are.

# THE PASSIONATE PAGAN AND THE
# DISPASSIONATE PUBLIC

### A TRAGEDY OF THE MACHINE AGE

Boys and girls,
Come out to play,
The moon is shining
Bright as day.

*If the moon is shining*
*Bright as day,*
*We think that we'll*
*Stay in and play.*

Hey nonny nonny!
Come, Jennie! Come, Johnnie!
The year's adolescent!
The air's effervescent!
It bubbles like Schweppes!
Aren't you going to take steppes?

*It's one of the commoner*
*Vernal phenomena.*
*You may go wild*
*Over air that is mild,*
*But Johnnie and Jennie*
*Are not having any.*

It is Spring! It is Spring!
Let us leap! Let us sing!
Let us claim we have hives
And abandon our wives!
Let us hire violins
To encourage our sins!
Let us loll in a grotto!
Let this be our motto:
Not sackcloth, but satin!
Not Nordic, but Latin!

*An epicene voice*
*Is our amorous choice!*
*Tell us that Luna*
*Compares with that cruna.*
*Away with your capers!*
*Go peddle your papers!*

It is Spring! It is Spring!
On the lea, on the ling!
The frost is dispersed!
Like the buds let us burst!
Let the sap in our veins
Rush like limited trains!
Let our primitive urges
Disgruntle our clergies,
While Bacchus and Pan
Cavort in the van!

*Spring is what winter*
*Always goes inter.*
*Science finds reasons*
*For mutable seasons.*
*Can't you control*
*That faun in your soul?*
*Please go and focus*
*Your whims on a crocus.*

It is Spring! Is it Spring?
Let us sing! Shall we sing?
On the lea, on the ling
Shall we sing it is Spring?
Will nobody fling
A garland to Spring?
Oh, hey nonny nonny!
Oh, Jennie! Oh, Johnnie!
Doesn't dove rhyme with love
While the moon shines above?
Isn't May for the wooer
And June for *l'amour?*

No, it couldn't be Spring!
Do not dance! Do not sing!
These birds and these flowers,
These breezes and bowers,
These gay tirra-lirras
Are all done with mirrors!
Hey nonny! Hey nonny!
Hey nonny! Hey nonny!
Hey nonny! Hey nonny!
Hey nonny . . .

---

## THEATRICAL REFLECTION

In the Vanities
No one wears panities.

---

## PORTRAIT OF THE ARTIST AS A PREMATURELY OLD MAN

It is common knowledge to every schoolboy and even every
    Bachelor of Arts,
That all sin is divided into two parts.
One kind of sin is called a sin of commission, and that is very
    important,
And it is what you are doing when you are doing something
    you ortant,
And the other kind of sin is just the opposite and is called a
    sin of omission and is equally bad in the eyes of all right-
    thinking people, from Billy Sunday to Buddha,
And it consists of not having done something you shuddha.
I might as well give you my opinion of these two kinds of

sin as long as, in a way, against each other we are pitting
them,
And that is, don't bother your head about sins of commission
because however sinful, they must at least be fun or else
you wouldn't be committing them.
It is the sin of omission, the second kind of sin,
That lays eggs under your skin.
The way you get really painfully bitten
Is by the insurance you haven't taken out and the checks you
haven't added up the stubs of and the appointments you
haven't kept and the bills you haven't paid and the letters
you haven't written.
Also, about sins of omission there is one particularly painful
lack of beauty,
Namely, it isn't as though it had been a riotous red-letter day
or night every time you neglected to do your duty;
You didn't get a wicked forbidden thrill
Every time you let a policy lapse or forgot to pay a bill;
You didn't slap the lads in the tavern on the back and loudly
cry Whee,
Let's all fail to write just one more letter before we go home,
and this round of unwritten letters is on me.
No, you never get any fun
Out of the things you haven't done,
But they are the things that I do not like to be amid,
Because the suitable things you didn't do give you a lot more
trouble than the unsuitable things you did.
The moral is that it is probably better not to sin at all, but
if some kind of sin you must be pursuing,
Well, remember to do it by doing rather than by not doing.

## TABOO TO BOOT

One bliss for which
There is no match
Is when you itch
To up and scratch.

Yet doctors and dowagers deprecate scratching,
Society ranks it with spitting and snatching,
And medical circles consistently hold
That scratching's as wicked as feeding a cold.
Hell's flame burns unquenched 'neath how many a stocking
On account of to scratch in a salon is shocking!

'Neath tile or thatch
That man is rich
Who has a scratch
For every itch.

Ho, squirmers and writhers, how long will ye suffer
The medical tyrant, the social rebuffer!
On the edge of the door let our shoulder blades rub,
Let the drawing room now be as free as the tub!

I'm greatly attached
To Barbara Frietchie.
I bet she scratched
When she was itchy.

---

## ADVICE OUTSIDE A CHURCH

Dead George, behold the portentous day
When bachelorhood is put away.
Bring camphor balls and cedarwood
For George's discarded bachelorhood;

You, as the happiest of men,
Wish not to wear it ever again.
Well, if you wish to get your wish,
Mark well my words, nor reply Tush-pish.
Today we fly, tomorrow we fall,
And lawyers make bachelors of us all.
If you desire a noisy nursery
And a golden wedding anniversary,
Scan first the bog where thousands falter:
They think the wooing ends at the altar,
And boast that one triumphant procession
Has given them permanent possession.
They simply desist from further endeavor,
And assume that their brides are theirs forever.
They do not beat them, they do no wrong to them,
But they take it for granted their brides belong to them.
Oh, every trade develops its tricks,
Marriage as well as politics,
Suspense is silk and complacence is shoddy,
And no one belongs to anybody.
It is pleasant, George, and necessary
To pretend the arrangement is temporary.
Thank her kindly for favors shown;
She is the lender, and she the loan;
Nor appear to notice the gradual shift
By which the loan becomes a gift.
Strong are the couples who resort
More to courtship and less to court.
And I warn you, George, for your future good,
That ladies don't want to be understood.
Women are sphinxes, Woman has writ it;
If you understand her, never admit it.
Tell her that Helen was probably beautifuller,
Call, if you will, Penelope dutifuller,
Sheba charminger, Guinevere grander
But never admit that you understand her.
Hark to the strains of Lohengrin!
Heads up, George! Go in and win!

# OUR CHILD DOESN'T KNOW ANYTHING
## or
## THANK GOD!

I am now about to make a remark that I suppose most parents
 will think me hateful for,
Though as a matter of fact I am only commenting on a condition that they should be more than grateful for.
What I want to say is, that of luckiness it seems to me to be
 the height
That babies aren't very bright.
Now listen to me for a minute, all you proud progenitors who
 boast that your bedridden infant offspring of two months
 or so are already bright enough to get into Harvard or
 Stanford or Notre Dame or Fordham;
Don't you realize that the only thing that makes life at all
 bearable to those selfsame offspring is being rather back-
 ward, and that if they had any sense at all they would
 lose no time in perishing of boredom?
Good heavens, I can think of no catastrophe more immense
Than a baby with sense,
Because one thing at least, willy-nilly, you must believe,
And that is, that a baby has twenty-four hours a day to get
 through with just the same as we've.
Some people choose to wonder about virtue and others about
 crime,
But I choose to wonder how babies manage to pass the time.
They can't pass it in tennis or badminton or golf,
Or in going around rescuing people from Indians and then
 marrying somebody else the way Pocahontas did with
 the Messrs. Smith and Rolfe;
They can't pass it in bridge or parchesi or backgammon,
Or in taking the subway to Wall Street and worshipping
 Mammon;
How then do they manage to enthuse themselves,
And amuse themselves?
Well, partly they sleep,
And mostly they weep,
And the rest of the time they relax

On their backs,
And eat, by régime specifically, but by nature omnivorously,
And vocalize vocivorously.
That, to make it short,
Is about all they can do in the way of sport;
So whatever may come,
I am glad that babies are dumb.
I shudder to think what for entertainment they would do
Were they as bright as me or you.

---

## LISTEN . . .

There is a knocking in the skull,
An endless silent shout
Of something beating on a wall,
And crying, Let me out.

That solitary prisoner
Will never hear reply,
No comrade in eternity
Can hear the frantic cry.

No heart can share the terror
That haunts his monstrous dark;
The light that filters through the chinks
No other eye can mark.

When flesh is linked with eager flesh,
And words run warm and full,
I think that he is loneliest then,
The captive in the skull.

Caught in a mesh of living veins,
In cell of padded bone,
He loneliest is when he pretends
That he is not alone.

We'd free the incarcerate race of man
That such a doom endures
Could only you unlock my skull,
Or I creep into yours.

---

## LOVE UNDER THE REPUBLICANS
### (OR DEMOCRATS)

Come live with me and be my love
And we will all the pleasures prove
Of a marriage conducted with economy
In the Twentieth Century Anno Donomy.
We'll live in a dear little walk-up flat
With practically room to swing a cat
And a potted cactus to give it hauteur
And a bathtub equipped with dark brown water.
We'll eat, without undue discouragement
Foods low in cost but high in nouragement
And quaff with pleasure, while chatting wittily,
The peculiar wine of Little Italy.
We'll remind each other it's smart to be thrifty
And buy our clothes for something-fifty.
We'll stand in line on holidays
For seats at unpopular matinees,
And every Sunday we'll have a lark
And take a walk in Central Park.
And one of these days not too remote
I'll probably up and cut your throat.

# DON'T CRY, DARLING, IT'S BLOOD ALL RIGHT

Whenever poets want to give you the idea that something is
    particularly meek and mild,
They compare it to a child,
Thereby proving that though poets with poetry may be rife
They don't know the facts of life.
If of compassion you desire either a tittle or a jot,
Don't try to get it from a tot.
Hard-boiled, sophisticated adults like me and you
May enjoy ourselves thoroughly with *Little Women* and
    *Winnie-the-Pooh*,
But innocent infants these titles from their reading course
    eliminate
As soon as they discover that it was honey and nuts and
    mashed potatoes instead of human flesh that Winnie-the-
    Pooh and Little Women ate.
Innocent infants have no use for fables about rabbits or don-
    keys or tortoises or porpoises,
What they want is something with plenty of well-mutilated
    corpoises.
Not on legends of how the rose came to be a rose instead of
    a petunia is their fancy fed,
But on the inside story of how somebody's bones got ground
    up to make somebody else's bread.
They'll go to sleep listening to the story of the little beggar-
    maid who got to be queen by being kind to the bees and
    the birds,
But they're all eyes and ears the minute they suspect a wolf
    or a giant is going to tear some poor woodcutter into
    quarters or thirds.
It really doesn't take much to fill their cup;
All they want is for somebody to be eaten up.
Therefore I say unto you, all you poets who are so crazy
    about meek and mild little children and their angelic
    air,
If you are sincere and really want to please them, why just
    go out and get yourselves devoured by a bear.

## MY DADDY

I have a funny daddy
Who goes in and out with me,
And everything that baby does
My daddy's sure to see,
And everything that baby says
My daddy's sure to tell.
You *must* have read my daddy's verse.
I hope he fries in hell.

---

## IT MUST BE THE MILK

There is a thought that I have tried not to but cannot help
    but think,
Which is, My goodness how much infants resemble people
    who have had too much to drink.
Tots and sots, so different and yet so identical!
What a humiliating coincidence for pride parentical!
Yet when you see your little dumpling set sail across the
    nursery floor,
Can you conscientiously deny the resemblance to somebody
    who is leaving a tavern after having tried to leave it a
    dozen times and each time turned back for just once
    more?
Each step achieved
Is simply too good to be believed;
Foot somehow follows foot
And somehow manages to stay put;
Arms wildly semaphore,
Wild eyes seem to ask, Whatever did we get in such a dilem-
    ma for?
And their gait is more that of a duckling than a Greek god-
    dessling or godling,

And in inebriates it's called staggering but in infants it's
    called toddling.
Another kinship with topers is also by infants exhibited,
Which is that they are completely uninhibited,
And they can't talk straight
Any more than they can walk straight;
Their pronunciation is awful
And their grammar is flawful,
And in adults it's drunken and maudlin and deplorable,
But in infants it's tunnin' and adorable.
So I hope you will agree that it is very hard to tell an infant
    from somebody who has gazed too long into the cup,
And really the only way you can tell them apart is to wait
    till next day, and the infant is the one that feels all right
    when it wakes up.

---

## A LADY THINKS SHE IS THIRTY

Unwillingly Miranda wakes,
Feels the sun with terror,
One unwilling step she takes,
Shuddering to the mirror.

Miranda in Miranda's sight
Is old and gray and dirty;
Twenty-nine she was last night;
This morning she is thirty.

Shining like the morning star,
Like the twilight shining,
Haunted by a calendar,
Miranda sits a-pining.

Silly girl, silver girl,
Draw the mirror toward you;

Time who makes the years to whirl
Adorned as he adored you.

Time is timelessness for you;
Calendars for the human;
What's a year, or thirty, to
Loveliness made woman?

Oh, Night will not see thirty again,
Yet soft her wing, Miranda;
Pick up your glass and tell me, then—
How old is Spring, Miranda?

––––––––––

## EDOUARD

A bugler named Dougal MacDougal
Found ingenious ways to be frugal.
He learned how to sneeze
In various keys,
Thus saving the price of a bugle.

––––––––––

## IN WHICH THE POET IS ASHAMED BUT PLEASED

Of all the things that I would rather,
It is to be my daughter's father,
While she, with innocence divine,
Is quite contented to be mine.

I am distressingly aware
That this arrangement is unfair,

For I, when in my celibate garrison,
Acquired some standard of comparison.

I visited nurseries galore,
Compiled statistics by the score,
And gained experience from a crew
Of children passing in review.

I saw the best that parents vaunted;
They weren't exactly what I wanted;
Yet, all the offspring that I faced,
They served to cultivate my taste.

Thus, let the miser praise the mintage,
And let the vintner praise the vintage;
I'm conscious that in praising her,
I'm speaking as a connoisseur.

While she, poor dear, has never known
A father other than her own.
She wots of other girls' papas
No more than of the Persian Shah's.

Within her head no notion stirs
That some are better men than hers;
That some are richer, some are kinder,
Some are solider, some refineder,

That some are vastly more amusing,
Some fitter subjects for enthusing,
That some are cleverer, some are braver,
Than the one that fortune gave her.

What fortune set us side by side,
Her scope so narrow, mine so wide?
We owe to this sweet dispensation
Our mutual appreciation.

# I KNOW YOU'LL LIKE THEM

You don't need to study any ponderous tome
To find out how to make your out-of-town guests feel not at
      home,
Because there is one way which couldn't be exquisiter
For enthralling the visitor.
You plan a little gathering informal and sociable
And you ask a few friends whose manners are irreproaciable,
And you speak up with all the pride of Mr. Dewey an-
      nouncing a couple of important impending arrests,
And you say, Friends, this is Mr. and Mrs. Comfitmonger, my
      out-of-town guests,
And you even amplify your introduction so as to break the
      ice with more velocity,
And you tell them that Mrs. Comfitmonger used to be a
      policewoman and Mr. Comfitmonger is a piano tuner of
      no mean virtuosity,
And you hint that Mr. Comfitmonger has had some pretty in-
      triguing experiences in his years as a virtuoso,
And that Mrs. Comfitmonger while pounding her beat has
      dealt with personalities who would scare the pants off
      Lombroso,
And that everything is all set for a dandy evening of general
      chit-chat is what you think,
And you retire to the pantry to prepare everybody a drink,
And you hear the brouhaha of vivacious voices,
And your heart rejoices,
Because it seems that your friends find Mr. Comfitmonger's
      anecdotes of life inside the Steinways fascinating,
And are spellbound by Mrs. Comfitmonger's articulate opposi-
      tion to arson and assassinating,
And you say This party is indeed de luxe,
And you emerge to find all your friends excitedly discussing
      putts that wouldn't go down and stocks that wouldn't
      go up, and Mr. and Mrs. Comfitmonger over in a corner
      leafing through your books,
And if you think you can turn the conversation to Palestrina
      or police work,

You've taken on a mighty pretty job of piecework,
Because if there is one thing in which everybody's home-team
    friends are unerring,
It is to confine their conversation to mutual acquaintances
    and episodes as to which your visiting friends have no
    idea of to what they are referring.
Most people are only vocal
When talking local.

---

## THE CANARY

The song of canaries
Never varies,
And when they're moulting
They're pretty revolting.

---

## THE TERRIBLE PEOPLE

People who have what they want are very fond of telling
    people who haven't what they want that they really don't
    want it,
And I wish I could afford to gather all such people into a
    gloomy castle on the Danube and hire half a dozen ca-
    pable Draculas to haunt it.
I don't mind their having a lot of money, and I don't care
    how they employ it,
But I do think that they damn well ought to admit they enjoy
    it.
But no, they insist on being stealthy
About the pleasures of being wealthy,
And the possession of a handsome annuity

Makes them think that to say how hard it is to make both
　　ends meet is their bounden duity.
You cannot conceive of an occasion
Which will find them without some suitable evasion.
Yes indeed, with arguments they are very fecund;
Their first point is that money isn't everything, and that they
　　have no money anyhow is their second.
Some people's money is merited,
And other people's is inherited,
But wherever it comes from,
They talk about it as if it were something you got pink gums
　　from.
Perhaps indeed the possession of wealth is constantly distress-
　　ing,
But I should be quite willing to assume every curse of wealth
　　if I could at the same time assume every blessing.
The only incurable troubles of the rich are the troubles that
　　money can't cure,
Which is a kind of trouble that is even more troublesome if
　　you are poor.
Certainly there are lots of things in life that money won't buy,
　　but it's very funny—
Have you ever tried to buy them without money?

---

## THE TALE OF CUSTARD THE DRAGON

Belinda lived in a little white house,
With a little black kitten and a little gray mouse,
And a little yellow dog and a little red wagon,
And a realio, trulio, little pet dragon.

Now the name of the little black kitten was Ink,
And the little gray mouse, she called her Blink,
And the little yellow dog was sharp as Mustard,
But the dragon was a coward, and she called him Custard.

[ 80 ]

Custard the dragon had big sharp teeth,
And spikes on top of him and scales underneath,
Mouth like a fireplace, chimney for a nose,
And realio, trulio daggers on his toes.

Belinda was as brave as a barrel full of bears,
And Ink and Blink chased lions down the stairs,
Mustard was as brave as a tiger in a rage,
But Custard cried for a nice safe cage.

Belinda tickled him, she tickled him unmerciful,
Ink, Blink and Mustard, they rudely called him Percival,
They all sat laughing in the little red wagon
At the realio, trulio, cowardly dragon.

Belinda giggled till she shook the house,
And Blink said Weeck! which is giggling for a mouse,
Ink and Mustard rudely asked his age,
When Custard cried for a nice safe cage.

Suddenly, suddenly they heard a nasty sound,
And Mustard growled, and they all looked around.
Meowch! cried Ink, and Ooh! cried Belinda.
For there was a pirate, climbing in the winda.

Pistol in his left hand, pistol in his right,
And he held in his teeth a cutlass bright,
His beard was black, one leg was wood;
It was clear that the pirate meant no good.

Belinda paled, and she cried Help! Help!
But Mustard fled with a terrified yelp,
Ink trickled down to the bottom of the household,
And little mouse Blink strategically mouseholed.

But up jumped Custard, snorting like an engine,
Clashed his tail like irons in a dungeon,
With a clatter and a clank and a jangling squirm
He went at the pirate like a robin at a worm.

The pirate gaped at Belinda's dragon,
And gulped some grog from his pocket flagon,
He fired two bullets, but they didn't hit,
And Custard gobbled him, every bit.

Belinda embraced him, Mustard licked him,
No one mourned for his pirate victim.
Ink and Blink in glee did gyrate
Around the dragon that ate the pyrate.

But presently up spoke little dog Mustard,
I'd have been twice as brave if I hadn't been flustered.
And up spoke Ink and up spoke Blink,
We'd have been three times as brave, we think,
And Custard said, I quite agree
That everybody is braver than me.

Belinda still lives in her little white house,
With her little black kitten and her little gray mouse,
And her little yellow dog and her little red wagon,
And her realio, trulio, little pet dragon.

Belinda is as brave as a barrel full of bears,
And Ink and Blink chase lions down the stairs,
Mustard is as brave as a tiger in a rage,
But Custard keeps crying for a nice safe cage.

---

## POLITICAL REFLECTION

Like an art-lover looking at the Mona Lisa in the Louvre
Is the *New York Herald Tribune* looking at Mr. Herbert
    Houvre.

# THE BIG TENT UNDER THE ROOF

Noises new to sea and land
Issue from the circus band.
Each musician looks like mumps
From blowing umpah umpah umps.

Lovely girls in spangled pants
Ride on gilded elephants.
Elephants are useful friends,
They have handles on both ends;
They hold each other's hindmost handles
And flee from mice and Roman candles.
Their hearts are gold, their hides are emery,
And they have a most tenacious memory.

Notice also, girls and boys,
The circus horses' avoirdupois.
Far and wide the wily scouts
Seek these snow-white stylish stouts.
Calmer steeds were never found
Unattached to a merry-go-round.
Equestriennes prefer to jump
Onto horses pillow-plump.

Equestriennes will never ride
As other people do, astride.
They like to balance on one foot,
And wherever they get, they won't stay put.
They utter frequent whoops and yips,
And have the most amazing hips.
Pink seems to be their favorite color,
And very few things are very much duller.

Yet I for one am more than willing
That everything should be less thrilling.
My heart and lungs both bound and balk
When high-wire walkers start to walk.

They ought to perish, yet they don't;
Some fear they will, some fear they won't.

I lack the adjectives, verbs and nouns
To do full justice to the clowns.
Their hearts are constantly breaking, I hear,
And who am I to interfere?
I'd rather shake hands with Mr. Ringling
And tell him his circus is a beautiful thingling.

---

## TWO AND ONE ARE A PROBLEM

Dear Miss Dix, I am a young man of half-past thirty-seven.
My friends say I am not unattractive, though to be kind and
    true is what I have always striven.
I am open-minded about beverages so long as they are grape,
    brandy or malt,
And I am generous to practically any fault.
Well Miss Dix not to beat around the bush, there is a certain
    someone who thinks I am pretty nice,
And I turn to you for advice.
You see, it started when I was away on the road
And returned to find a pair of lovebirds had taken up their
    residence in my abode.
Well I am not crazy about lovebirds, but I must say they
    looked very sweet in their gilded cage,
And their friendship had reached an advanced stage,
And I had just forgiven her who of the feathered fiancés was
    the donor of
When the children caught a lost lovebird in the yard that we
    couldn't locate the owner of.
So then we had three, and it was no time for flippancy,
Because everybody knows that a lovebird without its own
    lovebird to love will pine way and die of the discrepancy,

So we bought a fourth lovebird for the third lovebird and they
    sat around very cozily beak to beak
And then the third lovebird that we had provided the fourth
    lovebird for to keep it from dying died at the end of the
    week,
So we were left with an odd lovebird and it was no time for
    flippancy,
Because a lovebird without its own lovebird to love will pine
    away and die of the discrepancy,
So we had to buy a fifth lovebird to console the fourth love-
    bird that we had bought to keep the third lovebird con-
    tented,
And now the fourth lovebird has lost its appetite, and Miss
    Dix, I am going demented.
I don't want to break any hearts, but I got to know where
    I'm at;
Must I keep on buying lovebirds, Miss Dix, or do you think
    it would be all right to buy a cat?

---

## THUNDER OVER THE NURSERY

Listen to me, angel tot,
Whom I love an awful lot,
It will save a barrel of bother
If we understand each other.

Every time that I'm your herder
You think you get away with murder.
All right, infant, so you do,
But only because I want you to.

Baby's muscles are prodigious,
Baby's beautiful, not higious,
She can talk and walk and run
Like a daughter of a gun.

Well, you may be a genius, child,
And I a parent dull and mild;
In spite of which, and nevertheless,
I could lick you yet, I guess.

Forgive me, pet, if I am frank,
But truth is money in the bank;
I wish you to admire and love yourself,
But not to get too far above yourself.

When we race, you always win;
Baby, think before you grin.
It may occur to you, perhaps,
That Daddy's running under wraps.

When you hide behind the chair
And Daddy seeks you everywhere,
Behind the door, beneath the bed—
That's Daddy's heart, not Baby's head.

When I praise your speech in glee
And claim you talk as well as me,
That's the spirit, not the letter.
I know more words, and say them better.

In future, then, when I'm your herder,
Continue getting away with murder;
But know from him who murder endures,
It's his idea much more than yours.

———————

## MR. ARTESIAN'S CONSCIENTIOUSNESS

Once there was a man named Mr. Artesian and his activity
   was tremendous,
And he grudged every minute away from his desk because the
   importance of his work was so stupendous;

And he had one object all sublime,
Which was to save simply oodles of time.
He figured that sleeping eight hours a night meant that if he
lived to be seventy-five he would have spent twenty-five
years not at his desk but in bed,
So he cut his slumber to six hours which meant he only lost
eighteen years and nine months instead,
And he figured that taking ten minutes for breakfast and
twenty minutes for luncheon and half an hour for dinner
meant that he spent three years, two months and fifteen
days at the table,
So that by subsisting solely on bouillon cubes which he
swallowed at his desk to save this entire period he was
able,
And he figured that at ten minutes a day he spent a little over
six months and ten days shaving,
So he grew a beard, which gave him a considerable saving,
And you might think that now he might have been satisfied,
but no, he wore a thoughtful frown,
Because he figured that at two minutes a day he would spend
thirty-eight days and a few minutes in elevators just
traveling up and down,
So as a final timesaving device he stepped out the window of
his office, which happened to be on the fiftieth floor,
And one of his partners asked "Has he vertigo?" and the other
glanced out and down and said "Oh no, only about ten
feet more."

---

## THE LAMA

The one-l lama,
He's a priest,
The two-l llama,
He's a beast.
And I will bet

A silk pajama
There isn't any
Three-l lllama.*


---


## FAMILY COURT

One would be in less danger
From the wiles of the stranger
If one's own kin and kith
Were more fun to be with.


---


## THE GERM

A mighty creature is the germ,
Though smaller than the pachyderm.
His customary dwelling place
Is deep within the human race.
His childish pride he often pleases
By giving people strange diseases.
Do you, my poppet, feel infirm?
You probably contain a germ.


---


## THE COW

The cow is of the bovine ilk;
One end is moo, the other, milk.

* The author's attention has been called to a type of conflagration known as the three-alarmer. Pooh.

# THE MIND OF PROFESSOR PRIMROSE

My story begins in the town of Cambridge, Mass.,
Home of the Harvard Business and Dental Schools,
And more or less the home of Harvard College.
Now, Harvard is a cultural institution,
Squandering many a dollar upon professors,
As a glance at a Harvard football team makes obvious;
Professors wise and prowling in search of wisdom,
And every mother's son of them absent-minded.
But the absentest mind belonged to Professor Primrose.
He had won a Nobel award and a Pulitzer Prize,
A Guggenheim and a leg on the Davis Cup,
But he couldn't remember to shave both sides of his face.
He discharged the dog and took the cook for an airing;
He frequently lit his hair and combed his cigar;
He set a trap for the baby and dandled the mice;
He wound up his key and opened the door with his watch;
He tipped his students and flunked the traffic policeman;
He fed the mosquitoes crumbs and slapped at the robins;
He always said his prayers when he entered the theater,
And left the church for a smoke between the acts;
He mixed the exterminator man a cocktail
And told his guests to go way, he had no bugs;
He rode the streets on a bicycle built for two,
And he never discovered he wasn't teaching at Yale.
At last one summer he kissed his crimson flannels
And packed his wife in camphor, and she complained.
She had always hated camphor, and she complained.
"My dear," she ordered, "these *contretemps* must cease;
You must bring this absent mind a little bit nearer;
You must tidy up that disorderly cerebellum;
You must write today and enroll in the Pelman Institute."
He embraced his pen and he took his wife in hand,
He wrinkled a stamp and thoughtfully licked his brow,
He wrote the letter and mailed it, and what do you know?
In a couple of days he disappeared from Cambridge.
"For heaven's sake, my husband has disappeared,"
Said Mrs. Primrose. "Now isn't that just like him?"

And she cut the meat and grocery orders in half,
And moved the chairs in the living room around,
And settled down to a little solid comfort.
She had a marvelous time for seven years,
At the end of which she took a train to Chicago.
She liked to go to Chicago once in a while
Because of a sister-in-law who lived in Cambridge.
Her eye was caught at Schenectady by the porter;
She noticed that he was brushing off a dime,
And trying to put the passenger in his pocket.
"Porter," she said, "aren't you Professor Primrose?
Aren't you my husband, the missing Professor Primrose?
And what did you learn at the Pelman Institute?"
"Good Lawd, Maria," the porter said, "good Lawd!
Did you say *Pelman?* Ah wrote to de *Pullman* folks!"

---

## REFLECTION ON INGENUITY

Here's a good rule of thumb:
Too clever is dumb.

---

## ELECTION DAY IS A HOLIDAY

People on whom I do not bother to dote
Are people who do not bother to vote.
Heaven forbid that they should ever be exempt
From contumely, obloquy and various kinds of contempt.
Some of them like Toscanini and some like Rudy Vallée,
But all of them take about as much interest in their right to
    ballot as their right to ballet.
They haven't voted since the heyday of Miss Russell (Lillian)

And excuse themselves by saying What's the difference of one
    vote in fifty million?
They have such refined and delicate palates
That they can discover no one worthy of their ballots,
And then when someone terrible gets elected
They say, There, that's just what I expected!
And they go around for four years spouting discontented
    criticisms
And contented witticisms,
And then when somebody to oppose the man they oppose gets
    nominated
They say Oh golly golly he's the kind of man I've always
    abominated,
And they have discovered that if you don't take time out to
    go to the polls
You can manage very nicely to get through thirty-six holes.
Oh let us cover these clever people very conspicuously with
    loathing,
For they are un-citizens in citizens' clothing.
They attempt to justify their negligence
On the grounds that no candidate appeals to people of their
    integligence,
But I am quite sure that if Abraham Lincoln (Rep.) ran
    against Thomas Jefferson (Dem.)
Neither man would be appealing enough to squeeze a vote
    out of them.

---

## OLD MEN

People expect old men to die,
They do not really mourn old men.
Old men are different. People look
At them with eyes that wonder when . . .
People watch with unshocked eyes;
But the old men know when an old man dies.

# THE VERY UNCLUBBABLE MAN

I observe, as I hold my lonely course,
That nothing exists without a source.
Thus, oaks from acorns, lions from cubs,
And health and wealth from the proper clubs.
There are yacht clubs, golf clubs, clubs for luncheon,
Clubs for flowing bowl and puncheon,
Clubs for dancing, clubs for gambling,
Clubs for sociable Sunday ambling,
Clubs for imbibing literature,
And clubs for keeping the cinema pure,
Clubs for friendship, clubs for snobbery,
Clubs for smooth political jobbery.
As civilization onward reels,
It's clubs that grease the speeding wheels.

Alas!

Oh, everybody belongs to something,
But I don't belong to anything;
No, I don't belong to anything, any more than the miller of
    Dee,
And everything seems to belong
To people who belong to something,
But I don't belong to anything,
So nothing belongs to me.

Racquet, Knickerbocker, Union League,
Shriners parading without fatigue,
Oddfellows, Red Men, Woodmen of the World,
Solvent Moose and Elks dew-pearled,
Tammany tigers, Temperance doves,
Groups of various hates and loves,
Success is the thing they all have an air of,
Theirs are the summonses taken care of,
Theirs are the incomes but not the taxes,
Theirs are the sharpest, best-ground axes;
Millions of members of millions of bands,

Greeting fellow members with helping hands;
Good fellows all in incorporated hordes,
Prosperity is what they are moving towards.

Alas!

Oh, everybody belongs to something,
But I don't belong to anything;
Yes, I belong to nothing at all, from Kiwanis to the R.F.C.,
And everything definitely belongs
To people who belong to lots of things,
But I don't belong to anything,
So nothing belongs to me.

---

### PEDIATRIC REFLECTION

Many an infant that screams like a calliope
Could be soothed by a little attention to its diope.

---

### GOOD-BY, OLD YEAR, YOU OAF
#### or
### WHY DON'T THEY PAY THE BONUS?

Many of the three hundred and sixty-five days of the year are
    followed by dreadful nights but one night is by far, oh
    yes, by far the worst,
And that, my friends, is the night of December the thirty-first.
Man can never get it though his head that he is born to be
    not a creditor but a debtor;
Man always thinks the annual thought that just because last
    year was terrible next year is bound to be better.

[ 93 ]

Man is a victim of dope
In the incurable form of hope;
Man is a blemishless Pollyanna,
And is convinced that the advent of every New Year will
    place him in possession of a bumper crop of manna.
Therefore Man fills himself up with a lot of joie de vivre
And goes out to celebrate New Year's Ivre;
Therefore millions of respectable citizens who just a week
    before have been perfectly happy to sit at home and be
    cozily Christmas carolized
Consider it a point of honor to go out on the town and get
    themselves paralyzed;
Therefore the whistles blow toot toot and the bells ring ding
    ding and the confetti goes confetti confetti at midnight
    on the thirty-first of December,
And on January first the world is full of people who either
    can't and wish they could, or can and wish they couldn't
    remember.
They never seem to learn from experience;
They keep on doing it year after year from the time they are
    puling infants till they are doddering octogenerience.
My goodness, if there's anything in heredity and environment
How can people expect the newborn year to manifest any
    culture or refironment?
Every New Year is the direct descendant, isn't it, of a long
    line of proven criminals?
And you can't turn it into a philanthropist by welcoming it
    with cocktails and champagne any more successfully than
    with prayer books and hyminals.
Every new year is a country as barren as the old one, and it's
    no use trying to forage it;
Every new year is incorrigible; then all I can say is for
    heaven's sakes, why go out of your way to incorrage it?

# A CAROL FOR CHILDREN

God rest you, merry Innocents,
Let nothing you dismay,
Let nothing wound an eager heart
Upon this Christmas day.

Yours be the genial holly wreaths,
The stockings and the tree;
An aged world to you bequeaths
Its own forgotten glee.

Soon, soon enough come crueler gifts,
The anger and the tears;
Between you now there sparsely drifts
A handful yet of years.

Oh, dimly, dimly glows the star
Through the electric throng;
The bidding in temple and bazaar
Drowns out the silver song.

The ancient altars smoke afresh,
The ancient idols stir;
Faint in the reek of burning flesh
Sink frankincense and myrrh.

Gaspar, Balthazar, Melchior!
Where are your offerings now?
What greetings to the Prince of War,
His darkly branded brow?

Two ultimate laws alone we know,
The ledger and the sword—
So far away, so long ago,
We lost the infant Lord.

Only the children clasp His hand;
His voice speaks low to them,

And still for them the shining band
Wings over Bethlehem.

God rest you, merry Innocents,
While innocence endures.
A sweeter Christmas than we to ours
May you bequeath to yours.

---

## LEGAL REFLECTION

The postal authorities of the United States of America
Frown on Curiosa, Erotica and Esoterica,
Which is a break, I guess,
For stockholders of the American Railway Express.

---

## LUCY LAKE

Lawsamassy, for heaven's sake!
Have you never heard of Lucy Lake?
Lucy is fluffy and fair and cosy,
Lucy is like a budding posy.
Lucy speaks with a tiny lisp,
Lucy's mind is a will-o'-the-wisp.
Lucy is just as meek as a mouse,
Lucy lives in a darling house,
With a darling garden and darling fence,
And a darling faith in the future tense.
A load of hay, or a crescent moon,
And she knows that things will be better soon.
Lucy resigns herself to sorrow
In building character for tomorrow.

Lucy tells us to carry on,
It's always darkest before the dawn.
A visit to Lucy's bucks you up,
Helps you swallow the bitterest cup.
Lucy Lake is meek as a mouse.
Let's go over to Lucy's house,
*And let's lynch Lucy!*

———————

## SONG TO BE SUNG BY THE FATHER OF INFANT FEMALE CHILDREN

My heart leaps up when I behold
A rainbow in the sky;
Contrariwise, my blood runs cold
When little boys go by.
For little boys as little boys,
No special hate I carry,
But now and then they grow to men,
And when they do, they marry.
No matter how they tarry,
Eventually they marry.
And, swine among the pearls,
They marry little girls.

Oh, somewhere, somewhere, an infant plays,
With parents who feed and clothe him.
Their lips are sticky with pride and praise,
But I have begun to loathe him.
Yes, I loathe with a loathing shameless
This child who to me is nameless.
This bachelor child in his carriage
Gives never a thought to marriage,
But a person can hardly say knife
Before he will hunt him a wife.

I never see an infant (male),
A-sleeping in the sun,
Without I turn a trifle pale
And think Is *he* the one?
Oh, first he'll want to crop his curls,
And then he'll want a pony,
And then he'll think of pretty girls
And holy matrimony.
He'll put away his pony,
And sigh for matrimony.
A cat without a mouse
Is he without a spouse.

Oh, somewhere he bubbles bubbles of milk,
And quietly sucks his thumbs.
His cheeks are roses painted on silk,
And his teeth are tucked in his gums.
But alas, the teeth will begin to grow,
And the bubbles will cease to bubble;
Given a score of years or so,
The roses will turn to stubble.
He'll sell a bond, or he'll write a book,
And his eyes will get that acquisitive look,
And raging and ravenous for the kill,
He'll boldly ask for the hand of Jill.
This infant whose middle
Is diapered still
Will want to marry
My daughter Jill.

Oh sweet be his slumber and moist his middle!
My dreams, I fear, are infanticiddle.
A fig for embryo Lohengrins!
I'll open all of his safety pins,
I'll pepper his powder, and salt his bottle,
And give him readings from Aristotle.
Sand for his spinach I'll gladly bring,
And Tabasco sauce for his teething ring.
Then perhaps he'll struggle through fire and water
To marry somebody else's daughter.

# THE PHŒNIX

Deep in the study
Of eugenics
We find that fabled
Fowl, the Phœnix.
The wisest bird
As ever was,
Rejecting other
Mas and Pas,
It lays one egg,
Not ten or twelve,
And when it's hatched it,
Out pops itself.

---

# THE SEVEN SPIRITUAL AGES OF
# MRS. MARMADUKE MOORE

Mrs. Marmaduke Moore, at the age of ten
(Her name was Jemima Jevons then),
Was the quaintest of little country maids.
Her pigtails slapped on her shoulderblades;
She fed the chickens, and told the truth
And could spit like a boy through a broken tooth.
She could climb a tree to the topmost perch,
And she used to pray in the Methodist church.

At the age of twenty her heart was pure,
And she caught the fancy of Mr. Moore.
He broke his troth (to a girl named Alice),
And carried her off to his city palace,
Where she soon forgot her childhood piety
And joined in the orgies of high society.
Her voice grew English, or, say, Australian,
And she studied to be an Episcopalian.

At thirty our lives are still before us,
But Mr. Moore had a friend in the chorus.
Connubial bliss was overthrown
And Mrs. Moore now slumbered alone.
Hers was a nature that craved affection;
She gave herself up to introspection;
Then, finding theosophy rather dry,
Found peace in the sweet Bahai and Bahai.

Forty! and still an abandoned wife.
She felt old urges stirring to life.
She dipped her locks in a bowl of henna
And booked a passage through to Vienna.
She paid a professor a huge emolument
To demonstrate what his ponderous volume meant.
Returning, she preached to the unemployed
The gospel according to St. Freud.

Fifty! she haunted museums and galleries,
And pleased young men by augmenting their salaries.
Oh, it shouldn't occur, but it does occur,
That poets are made by fools like her.
Her salon was full of frangipani,
Roumanian, Russian and Hindustani,
And she conquered par as well as bogey
By reading a book and going Yogi.

Sixty! and time was on her hands—
Maybe remorse and maybe glands.
She felt a need for a free confession,
To publish each youthful indiscretion,
And before she was gathered to her mothers,
To compare her sinlets with those of others,
Mrs. Moore gave a joyous whoop,
And immersed herself in the Oxford Group.

That is the story of Mrs. Moore,
As far as it goes. But of this I'm sure—
When seventy stares her in the face

She'll have found some other state of grace.
Mohammed may be her Lord and master,
Or Zeus, or Mithros or Zoroaster.
When a lady's erotic life is vexed
God knows what God is coming next.

---

## WHAT ALMOST EVERY WOMAN KNOWS
## SOONER OR LATER

Husbands are things that wives have to get used to putting
    up with,
And with whom they breakfast with and sup with.
They interfere with the discipline of nurseries,
And forget anniversaries,
And when they have been particularly remiss
They think they can cure everything with a great big kiss,
And when you tell them about something awful they have
    done they just look unbearably patient and smile a
    superior smile,
And think, Oh she'll get over it after a while.
And they always drink cocktails faster than they can assimi-
    late them,
And if you look in their direction they act as if they were
    martyrs and you were trying to sacrifice, or immolate
    them.
And when it's a question of walking five miles to play golf
    they are very energetic but if it's doing anything useful
    around the house they are very lethargic,
And then they tell you that women are unreasonable and
    don't know anything about logic,
And they never want to get up or go to bed at the same time
    as you do,
And when you perform some simple common or garden rite
    like putting cold cream on your face or applying a

touch of lipstick they seem to think you are up to some kind of black magic like a priestess of Voodoo,

And they are brave and calm and cool and collected about the ailments of the person they have promised to honor and cherish,

But the minute they get a sniffle or a stomach-ache of their own, why you'd think they were about to perish,

And when you are alone with them they ignore all the minor courtesies and as for airs and graces, they utterly lack them,

But when there are a lot of people around they hand you so many chairs and ash trays and sandwiches and butter you with such bowings and scrapings that you want to smack them.

Husbands are indeed an irritating form of life,

And yet through some quirk of Providence most of them are really very deeply ensconced in the affection of their wife.

---

## SUPPOSE I DARKEN YOUR DOOR

It seems to me that if you must be sociable it is better to go and see people than to have people come and see you,

Because then you can leave when you are through.

Yes, the moment you begin to nod

You can look at your watch and exclaim Goodness gracious, it is ten o'clock already, I had no idea it was so late, how very odd!

And you politely explain that you have to get up early in the morning to keep an important engagement with a man from Alaska or Siam,

And you politely thank your host and hostess for the lovely time and politely say good night and politely scram,

But when you yourself are the home team and the gathering is under your own roof,

You haven't got a Manchurian's chance of being aloof.

If you glance at your watch it is grievous breach of hospitality and a disgrace,

And if you are caught in the midst of a yawn you have to pretend you were making a face and say Come on everybody, let's see who can make the funniest face.

Then as the evening wears on you feel more and more like an unsuccessful gladiator,

Because all the comfortable places to sit in are being sat in by guests and you have to repose on the window sill or the chandelier or the radiator,

And somebody has always brought along a girl who looks like a loaf of raisin bread and doesn't know anybody else in the room,

And you have to go over to the corner where she is moping and try to disperse her gloom,

And finally at last somebody gets up and says they have to get back to the country or back to town again,

And you feebly say Oh it's early, don't go yet, so what do they do but sit down again,

And people that haven't said a word all evening begin to get lively and people that have been lively all evening get their second wind and somebody says Let's all go out in the kitchen and scramble some eggs,

And you have to look at him or her twice before you can convince yourself that anybody who would make a suggestion like that hasn't two heads or three legs,

And by this time the birds are twittering in the trees or looking in the window and saying Boo,

But nobody does anything about it and as far as I know they're all still here, and that's the reason I say that it is better to go and see people than to have people come and see you.

# HUSH, HERE THEY COME

Some people get savage and bitter when to backbiters they
refer,
But I just purr.
Yes, some people consider backbiters to be rankest of the
rank,
But frankly, I prefer them to people who go around being
frank,
Because usually when you are backbitten behind your back
you don't know about it and it doesn't leave a trace,
But frankness consists of having your back bitten right to
your face,
And as if that weren't enough to scar you,
Why you are right there in person to scotch the defamation,
and if you don't happen to be able to scotch it, why
where are you?
Frank people are grim, but genuine backbiters are delightful
to have around.
Because they are so anxious that if what they have been say-
ing about you has reached your ears you shouldn't be-
lieve it, that they are the most amiable companions to
be found;
They will entertain you from sunset to dawn,
And cater encouragingly to all your weaknesses so that they
can broadcast them later on,
So what if they do gnaw on your spine after enjoying your
beer and skittles?
I don't blame them the least of jots or tittles,
Because certainly no pastime such diversion lends
As talking friends over analytically with friends,
So what if as they leave your house or you leave theirs back-
biters strip your flesh and your clothes off,
At least it is your back that they bite, and not your nose off.
I believe in a place for everything and everything in its place,
And I don't care how unkind the things people say about me
so long as they don't say them to my face.

# I YIELD TO MY LEARNED BROTHER
### or
# IS THERE A CANDLESTICK MAKER IN THE HOUSE?

The doctor gets you when you're born,
The preacher, when you marry,
And the lawyer lurks with costly clerks
If too much on you carry.
Professional men, they have no cares;
Whatever happens, they get theirs.

You can't say When
To professional men,
For it's always When to they;
They go out and golf
With the big bad wolf
In the most familiar way.
Hard times for them contain no terrors;
Their income springs from human errors.

The noblest lord is ushered in
By a practicing physician,
And the humblest lout is ushered out
By a certified mortician.
And in between, they find their foyers
Alive with summonses from lawyers.

Oh, would my parents long ago
Had memorized this motto!
For then might I, their offspring, buy
A Rolls or an Isotto.
But now I fear I never can,
For I am no professional man.

You can't say When
To professional men,
For it's always When to they;
They were doing fine

In '29,
And they're doing fine today.
One beacon doth their paths illumine,
To wit: To err is always humine.

---

## REFLECTION ON THE PASSAGE OF TIME, ITS INEVITABILITY AND ITS QUIRKS

In nineteen hundred
*Jeunes filles* wondered.

I'M A STRANGER HERE MYSELF

# CURL UP AND DIET

Some ladies smoke too much and some ladies drink too much
    and some ladies pray too much,
But all ladies think that they weigh too much.
They may be as slender as a sylph or a dryad,
But just let them get on the scales and they embark on a
    doleful jeremiad;
No matter how low the figure the needle happens to touch,
They always claim it is at least five pounds too much;
No matter how underfed to you a lady's anatomy seemeth,
She describes herself as Leviathan or Behemoth;
To the world she may appear slinky and feline,
But she inspects herself in the mirror and cries, Oh, I look
    like a sea lion.
Once upon a time there was a girl more beautiful and witty
    and charming than tongue can tell,
And she is now a dangerous raving maniac in a padded cell,
And the first indication her friends and relatives had that
    she was mentally overwrought
Was one day when she said, I weigh a hundred and twenty-
    seven, which is exactly what I ought.
Oh, often I am haunted
By the thought that somebody might some day discover a
    diet that would let ladies reduce just as much as they
    wanted,
Because I wonder if there is a woman in the world strong-
    minded enough to shed ten pounds or twenty,
And say There now, that's plenty;
And I fear me one ten-pound loss would only arouse the
    craving for another,
So it wouldn't do any good for ladies to get their ambition
    and look like somebody's fourteen-year-old brother,
Because, having accomplished this with ease,
They would next want to look like somebody's fourteen-year-
    old brother in the final stages of some obscure disease,
And the more success you have the more you want to get of it,
So then their goal would be to look like somebody's fourteen-

year-old brother's ghost, or rather not the ghost itself,
which is fairly solid, but a silhouette of it,
So I think it is very nice for ladies to be lithe and lissome,
But not so much so that you cut yourself if you happen to
embrace or kissome.

---

## BANKERS ARE JUST LIKE ANYBODY ELSE, EXCEPT RICHER

This is a song to celebrate banks,
Because they are full of money and you go into them and all
you hear is clinks and clanks,
Or maybe a sound like the wind in the trees on the hills,
Which is the rustling of the thousand dollar bills.
Most bankers dwell in marble halls,
Which they get to dwell in because they encourage deposits
and discourage withdralls,
And particularly because they all observe one rule which woe
betides the banker who fails to heed it,
Which is you must never lend any money to anybody unless
they don't need it.
I know you, you cautious conservative banks!
If people are worried about their rent it is your duty to deny
them the loan of a single penny, even though it be worth
only 3 7/10 francs.
Yes, if they request fifty dollars to pay for a baby you must
look at them like the English looking at Joan of Arc,
And tell them what do they think a bank is, anyhow, they
had better go get the money from their friendly neigh-
borhood shark.
But suppose people come in and they have a million and
they want another million to pile on top of it,
Why, you brim with the milk of human kindness and you
urge them to accept every drop of it,
And you lend them the million so then they have two million

and this gives them the idea that they would be better
off with four,
So they already have two million as security so you have no
hesitation in lending them two more,
And all the vice-presidents nod their heads in rhythm,
And the only question asked is do the borrowers want the
money sent or do they want to take it withm.
But please do not think that I am not fond of banks,
Because I think they deserve our appreciation and thanks,
Because they perform a valuable public service in eliminating
the jackasses who go around saying that health and
happiness are everything and money isn't essential,
Because as soon as they have to borrow some unimportant
money to maintain their health and happiness they
starve to death so they can't go around any more sneer-
ing at good old money, which is nothing short of provi-
dential.

---

## THE JAPANESE

How courteous is the Japanese;
He always says, "Excuse it, please."
He climbs into his neighbor's garden,
And smiles, and says, "I beg your pardon";
He bows and grins a friendly grin,
And calls his hungry family in;
He grins, and bows a friendly bow;
"So sorry, this my garden now."

# THE STRANGE CASE OF MR. DONNYBROOK'S BOREDOM

Once upon a time there was a man named Mr. Donnybrook.

∽

He was married to a woman named Mrs. Donnybrook.

∽

Mr. and Mrs. Donnybrook dearly loved to be bored.

∽

Sometimes they were bored at the ballet, other times at the cinema.

∽

They were bored riding elephants in India and elevators in the Empire State Building.

∽

They were bored in speakeasies during Prohibition and in cocktail lounges after Repeal.

∽

They were bored by Grand Dukes and garbagemen, debutantes and demimondaines, opera singers and operations.

∽

They scoured the Five Continents and the Seven Seas in their mad pursuit of boredom.

∽

This went on for years and years.

∽

One day Mr. Donnybrook turned to Mrs. Donnybrook.

∽

My dear, he said, we have reached the end of our rope.

We have exhausted every yawn.

∽

The world holds nothing more to jade our titillated palates.

∽

Well, said Mrs. Donnybrook, we might try insomnia.

∽

So they tried insomnia.

∽

About two o'clock the next morning Mr. Donnybrook said,
My, insomnia is certainly quite boring, isn't it?

∽

Mrs. Donnybrook said it certainly was, wasn't it?

∽

Mr. Donnybrook said it certainly was.

∽

Pretty soon he began to count sheep.

∽

Mrs. Donnybrook began to count sheep, too.

∽

After awhile Mr. Donnybrook said, Hey, you're counting my
sheep!

∽

Stop counting my sheep, said Mr. Donnybrook.

∽

Why, the very idea, said Mrs. Donnybrook.

∽

I guess I know my own sheep, don't I?

How? said Mr. Donnybrook.

∞

They're cattle, said Mrs. Donnybrook.

∞

They're cattle, and longhorns at that.

∞

Furthermore, said Mrs. Donnybrook, us cattle ranchers is
shore tired o' you sheepmen plumb ruinin' our water.

∞

I give yuh fair warnin', said Mrs. Donnybrook, yuh better git
them woolly Gila monsters o' yourn back across the Rio
Grande afore mornin' or I'm a goin' to string yuh up
on the nearest cottonwood.

∞

Carramba! sneered Mr. Donnybrook. Thees ees free range,
no?

∞

No, said Mrs. Donnybrook, not for sheepmen.

∞

She strung him up on the nearest cottonwood.

∞

Mr. Donnybrook had never been so bored in his life.

---

## TO A LADY PASSING TIME BETTER LEFT
## UNPASSED

O lady of the lucent hair,
Why do you play at solitaire?
What imp, what demon misanthrope,

Prompted this session of lonely hope?
What boredom drives you, and great Lord!
How can such as you be bored?
The gleaming world awaits your eye
While you essay futility.
That mouth is shaped for livelier sport
Than paging of a pasteboard court—
Why, even the Red Knave longing lingers,
While Black Queens wait, in those white fingers.—
See now the joy that lights your face
Squandered on some fortuitous ace,
Where formerly dark anger burned
When a five perverse would not be turned.
O, know you not, that darkling frown
Could topple Caesar's empire down;
That quick, bright joy, if flashed on men,
Could sudden build it up again?
Get up! Get up! Throw down the pack!
Rise in your gown of shining black!
Withdraw, my dear, while you are able
The slender feet from 'neath the table;
Remove from the regretful baize
The elbows curved in cunning ways.
Is there no game that pleasure brings
But fretting over painted things?
No gay, ecstatic end in view
But shuffle and begin anew?
Get up, I tell you, girl, get up!
Wine keeps not ever in the cup;
Even Love immortal, love undying,
Finds the loved one's Patience trying.
Let two-and-fifty rivals hiss me—
For God's sake, girl, come here and kiss me.

# NINE MILES TO THE RAILROAD

The country is a funny place,
I like to look it in the face.
And everywhere I look I see
Some kind of animal or tree.

Indeed, I frequently remark
The country is rather like a park.

The country cows give milk, and moo,
Just like their sisters in the zoo.
The rural squirrel in his rage
Chirks like a squirrel in a cage.

Animals, in their joys and passions,
Like women, follow city fashions.

The horses here pull plows and carts
All day until the sun departs.
In summer, or when fields are frosted,
They work until they are exhausted.

Next, to the track themselves they hie
To be bet upon by the likes of I.

As through the countryside you pass
You look at grass and still more grass.
Grass leers at you where'er you turn
Until your tired eyelids burn.

They ought to break it up, or soften it,
With pretty signs saying, please keep offen it.

I like the country very much.
It's good to hear and smell and touch.
It makes you feel akin with Nature,
Though wobbly on her nomenclature.

I'd free my lungs of city air
If I didn't feel much more important there.

# THE EIGHT O'CLOCK PERIL

Breakfast is an institution that I don't know who commenced it,

But I am not for it, I am against it.

It is a thoroughly inedible repast,

And the dictionary says it is derived from the words *break*, meaning *to break*, and *fast*, meaning a *fast*, so to break-fast means to break your fast.

Well that just shows how far you can trust a dictionary.

Because I never saw a definition that was more utterly fictionary.

The veriest child could see it doesn't check,

Because if the first syllable of breakfast means *to break*, why is it pronounced *brek?*

Shame on you, you old lexicographers, I shall call you laxicographers because you have grown very lax,

Because it is perfectly obvious that the first syllable in break-fast is derived from the far-famed Yale football cheer, which is Brekekekex co-ax co-ax,

And did you even get the second syllable right? Why a thousand times No,

Because the *fast* in *breakfast* doesn't mean fast, *abstinence from food*, it means *fast*, not *slow*.

So with that in mind we can peek behind the scenes

And then we can see what *break-fast* really means,

It means that if you wake up in the morning feeling unappetized and sickly,

Why you are confronted by a meal and the entire Yale football team coaxes you with an axe to eat it quickly.

# THE STRANGE CASE OF MR. BALLANTINE'S VALENTINE

Once upon a time there was an attorney named Mr. Ballantine.

∞

He lived in the spacious gracious days of the nineteenth century.

∞

Mr. Ballantine didn't know they were spacious and gracious.

∞

He thought they were terrible.

∞

The reason he thought they were terrible was that love had passed him by.

∞

Mr. Ballantine had never received a valentine.

∞

He said to his partner, My name is Mr. Ballantine and I have never received a valentine.

∞

His partner said, Well my name is Mr. Bogardus and I have received plenty of valentines and I just as soon wouldn't.

∞

He said Mr. Ballantine didn't know when he was well off.

∞

Mr. Ballantine said, I know my heart, I know my mind, I know I long for a valentine.

[ 118 ]

He said here it was St. Valentine's Day and when he sat down at his desk what did he find?

◇◇◇

Valentines?

◇◇◇

No.

◇◇◇

I find affidavits, said Mr. Ballantine.

◇◇◇

That's the kind of valentine I get, said Mr. Ballantine.

◇◇◇

Mr. Bogardus said that affidavit was better than no bread.

◇◇◇

Mr. Ballantine said that affidavit, affidavit, affidavit onward, into the valley of death rode the six hundred.

◇◇◇

Mr. Bogardus said that any man who would rhyme "onward" with "six hundred" didn't deserve any affidavits at all.

◇◇◇

Mr. Ballantine said coldly that he was an attorney, not a poet, and Mr. Bogardus had better take the matter up directly with Lord Tennyson.

◇◇◇

Mr. Bogardus said Oh all right, and speaking of lords, he couldn't remember who was the king before David, but Solomon was the king affidavit.

◇◇◇

Mr. Ballantine buried Mr. Bogardus in the cellar and went out in search of love.

[ 119 ]

Towards evening he enountered a maiden named Herculena, the Strongest Woman in the World.

∞

He said, Madam my name is Mr. Ballantine anl I have never received a valentine.

∞

Herculena was delighted.

∞

She said, My name is Herculena the Strongest Woman in the World, and I have never received a valentine either.

∞

Mr. Ballantine and Herculena decided to be each other's valentine.

∞

All was merry as a marriage bell.

∞

Mr. Ballantine nearly burst with joy.

∞

Herculena nearly burst with pride.

∞

She flexed her biceps.

∞

She asked Mr. Ballantine to pinch her muscle.

∞

Mr. Ballantine recovered consciousness just in time to observe the vernal equinox.

∞

He thought she said bustle.

# ONE MAN'S MEED IS ANOTHER MAN'S
# OVEREMPHASIS

I salute the section of our lordly Sunday journals which is
    entitled Scores of College Football Games Continued
    from Page One,
Because there a flock of not very notorious institutions of
    learning find their annual place in the sun.
Yes, the football season is a kindly time of year,
And during it we read of campuses of which at other times
    we do not often hear.
Would a playwright, for instance, ordinarily select Aurora
    as the Alma Mater for his hero?
Yet it is here recorded that Aurora one week held Wright Jr.
    to a six-to-six tie and the next week took the measure of
    Wartburg, nineteen to zero.
Yes, and the St. Cloud Teachers are an aggregation that no
    college-lover can conscientiously shelve,
Because they nosed out the Bemidji Teachers thirteen to
    twelve.
Oh ye of little faith who take Yale and Notre Dame for your
    Alpha and Omega,
What about Hiwassee, which outscored Biltmore, and Dillard,
    which engaged in a Homeric deadlock with Talladega?
When better endowments are offered,
Well, what's the matter with Augustana and Millsaps and
    Spearfish and Gustavus Adolphus and Wofford?
So if anybody makes derogatory remarks about the football
    season let us answer with scornful defiance,
And meanwhile let us not forget that Huron beat Yankton
    six to nothing on the very same day that Jamestown
    smothered Wahpeton Science.

# THE STRANGE CASE OF THE PLEASING
## TAXI–DRIVER

Once upon a time there was a taxi-driver named Llewellyn Abdullah—White—Male—5–10½—170.

☙

Llewellyn had promised his mother he would be the best taxi-driver in the world.

☙

His mother was in Heaven.

☙

At least, she was in a Fool's Paradise because her boy was the best taxi-driver in the world.

☙

He was, too.

☙

On rainy nights his flag was always up.

☙

He knew not only how to find the Waldorf, but the shortest route to 5954 Gorsuch Avenue.

☙

He said Thank you when tipped, and always had change for five dollars.

☙

He never drove with a cigar in his mouth, lighted or unlighted.

☙

If you asked him to please not drive so fast, he drove not so fast, and didn't get mad about it, either.

☙

He simply adored traffic cops, and he was polite to Sunday drivers.

When he drove a couple through the park he never looked back and he never eavesdropped.

∞

My boy is the best taxi-driver in the world and no eavesdropper, said his mother.

∞

The only trouble was that the bad taxi-drivers got all the business.

∞

Llewellyn shrank from White—Male—5–10½—170 to Sallow—Male—5–9¾—135.

∞

Cheest, Llewellyn, said his mother.

∞

Cheest, Mother, replied Llewellyn.

∞

Llewellyn and his mother understood each other.

∞

He took his last five dollars in dimes and nickels which he had been saving for change and spent it on cigars at two for a nickel.

∞

The next day he insulted seven passengers and a traffic cop, tore the fender off a car from Enid, Oklahoma, and passed through 125th Street while taking a dear old lady from 52nd to 58th.

∞

That evening he had forty dollars on the clock.

[ 123 ]

Llewellyn is no longer the best taxi-driver in the world, but his license reads White—Male—5–11—235.

∞

In the park he is the father of all eavesdroppers.

∞

Couples who protest find him adamant.

∞

Since he is the father of all eavesdroppers and adamant, I think we might call him an Adam-ant-Evesdropper and there leave him.

∞

Good-by, Llewellyn.

---

## THE STRANGE CASE OF THE AMBITIOUS CADDY

Once upon a time there was a boy named Robin Bideawee.

∞

He had chronic hiccups.

∞

He had hay fever, too.

∞

Also, he was learning to whistle through his teeth.

∞

Oh yes, and his shoes squeaked.

∞

The scoutmaster told him he had better be a caddy.

He said, Robin, you aren't cut out for a scout, you're cut out
for a caddy.

∞

At the end of Robin's first day as a caddy the caddymaster
asked him how he got along.

∞

Robin said, I got along fine but my man lost six balls, am I
ready yet?

∞

The caddymaster said No, he wasn't ready yet.

∞

At the end of the second day the caddymaster asked him
again how he got along.

∞

Robin said, My man left me behind to look for a ball on the
fourth hole and I didn't catch up to him till the eight-
eenth, am I ready yet?

∞

The caddymaster said No, he wasn't ready yet.

∞

Next day Robin said, I only remembered twice to take the
flag on the greens and when I did take it I wiggled it,
am I ready yet?

∞

The caddymaster said No, he wasn't ready yet.

∞

Next day Robin said, My man asked me whether he had a
seven or an eight on the waterhole and I said an eight,
am I ready yet?

The caddymaster said No, he wasn't ready yet.

∽

Next day Robin said, Every time my man's ball stopped on the edge of a bunker I kicked it in, am I ready yet?

∽

The caddymaster said No, he wasn't ready yet.

∽

Next day Robin said, I never once handed my man the club he asked for, am I ready yet?

∽

The caddymaster said No, he wasn't ready yet.

∽

Next day Robin said, I bet a quarter my man would lose and told him so, am I ready yet?

∽

The caddymaster said, Not quite.

∽

Next day Robin said, I laughed at my man all the way round, am I ready yet?

∽

The caddymaster said, Have you still got hiccups, and have you still got hay fever, and are you still learning how to whistle through your teeth and do your shoes still squeak?

∽

Robin said, Yes, yes, a thousand times yes.

∽

Then you are indeed ready, said the caddymaster.

∽

Tomorrow you shall caddy for Ogden Nash.

# I'M TERRIBLY SORRY FOR YOU, BUT I CAN'T HELP LAUGHING

Everybody has a perfect right to do what they please,
But one thing that I advise everybody not to do is to contract a laughable disease.
People speak of you respectfully if you catch bubonic,
And if you get typhus they think you have done something positively mastodonic;
One touch of leprosy makes the whole world your kin,
And even a slight concussion earns you an anxious inquiry and not a leering grin.
Yes, as long as people are pretty sure you have something you are going to be removed by,
Why they are very sympathetic, and books and flowers and visits and letters are what their sympathy is proved by.
But unfortunately there are other afflictions anatomical,
And people insist on thinking that a lot of them are comical,
And if you are afflicted with this kind of affliction people are amused and disdainful,
Because they are not bright enough to realize that an affliction can be ludicrous and still be ominous and painful.
Suppose for instance you have a dreadful attack of jaundice, what do they do?
They come around and smile and say Well well, how are you today, Dr. Fu-Manchu?
The early martyrs thought they knew what it was to be taken over the jumps,
But no martyr really ought to get his diploma until he has undergone his friends' witticisms during his mumps.
When you have laryngitis they rejoice,
Because apparently the funniest thing in the world is when you can't chide them for laughing at your lost voice, because you have lost your voice.
So I advise you, at the risk of being pedantic,
If you must be sick, by all means choose a sickness that is preferably fatal and certainly romantic,

Because it is much better to have that kind of sickness and
be sick unto death or anyway half to death,
Than to have the other kind and be laughed to death.

---

## THE STRANGE CASE OF THE GIRL
## O' MR. SPONSOON'S DREAMS

Once upon a time there was a man named Mr. Sponsoon
who was highly ineffectual.

∽

He always looked as if he were growing a moustache.

∽

His singing voice was pretty fair except for the high notes.

∽

Oh yes, and the low notes, too.

∽

One day he was driving along the street when he saw a beautiful girl.

∽

My, what a beautiful girl, said Mr. Sponsoon. I wish I knew
her name.

∽

If I asked her her name, said Mr. Sponsoon, she might think
me a brazen cad.

[ 128 ]

But if I don't know her name, she will go out of my life forever.

∽

Mr. Sponsoon thought and thought.

∽

Suppose I run over her gently, he thought at last.

∽

With one wheel, say.

∽

Certainly with no more than two.

∽

Then I can read her name in the morning paper and all will be hotsy-totsy.

∽

Mr. Sponsoon pointed his car at the beautiful girl.

∽

The beautiful girl leaped like a thoroughbred gazelle.

∽

Mr. Sponsoon chased her for seven blocks and never laid a wheel on her.

∽

In the middle of the eighth block she stopped to moisten her finger on account of a run in her stocking.

∽

Mr. Sponsoon read in the morning paper that her name was Shella Schminck and she was in Percy's Hospital.

∽

So he went to the Mercy Hospital and asked for Stella Smith.

To the girl o' his dreams he explained his little stratagem.

∽

Girl o' my dreams, I had to know your name, said Mr. Sponsoon, avoiding high notes and low notes.

∽

Say you forgive me, girl o' my dreams,

∽

Say all is hotsy-totsy.

∽

The girl o' Mr. Sponsoon's dreams said all was far from hotsy-totsy.

∽

All was coldsy-toldsy, said the girl o' Mr. Sponsoon's dreams.

∽

Mr. Sponsoon joined the Foreign Legion to forget.

∽

He did forget.

∽

He forgot it was the Foreign Legion.

∽

He thought it was the American Legion.

∽

Mr. Sponsoon applied a battery tickler-upper to the person of the favorite wife of an intransigent Sheikh.

∽

And so we bid farewell to Mr. Sponsoon.

## OH, PLEASE DON'T GET UP!

There is one form of life to which I unconditionally surrender,
Which is the feminine gender.
I think there must be some great difference in the way men
    and women are built,
Because women walk around all day wearing shoes that a
    man would break his neck the first step he took in them
    because where a man's shoe has a heel a woman's shoe
    has a stilt.
Certainly a man shod like a woman would just have to sit
    down all day, and yet my land!
Women not only don't have to sit, but prefer to stand,
Because their pleasure in standing up is exquisite,
As everybody knows who has ever watched a woman pay a
    call or a visit,
Because the proportions of feminine social chitchat are con-
    stant, always;
One part of sitting down in the sitting room to four parts
    standing up saying good-by in foyers and hallways,
Which is why I think that when it comes to physical prowess,
Why woman is a wow, or should I say a wowess.

---

## JUST KEEP QUIET AND NOBODY WILL NOTICE

There is one thing that ought to be taught in all the colleges,
Which is that people ought to be taught not to go around
    always making apologies.
I don't mean the kind of apologies people make when they
    run over you or borrow five dollars or step on your feet,
Because I think that kind is sort of sweet;
No, I object to one kind of apology alone,
Which is when people spend their time and yours apologiz-
    ing for everything they own.
You go to their house for a meal,

And they apologize because the anchovies aren't caviar or the partridge is veal;
They apologize privately for the crudeness of the other guests,
And they apologize publicly for their wife's housekeeping or their husband's jests;
If they give you a book by Dickens they apologize because it isn't by Scott,
And if they take you to the theater, they apologize for the acting and the dialogue and the plot;
They contain more milk of human kindness than the most capacious dairy can,
But if you are from out of town they apologize for everything local and if you are a foreigner they apologize for everything American.
I dread these apologizers even as I am depicting them,
I shudder as I think of the hours that must be spent in contradicting them,
Because you are very rude if you let them emerge from an argument victorious,
And when they say something of theirs is awful, it is your duty to convince them politely that it is magnificent and glorious,
And what particularly bores *me* with them,
Is that half the time you have to politely contradict them when you rudely agree with them,
So I think there is one rule every host and hostess ought to keep with the comb and nail file and bicarbonate and aromatic spirits on a handy shelf,
Which is don't spoil the denouement by telling the guests everything is terrible, but let them have the thrill of finding it out for themself.

# LINES TO BE SCRIBBLED ON SOMEBODY
## ELSE'S THIRTIETH MILESTONE

Thirty today? Cheer up, my lad!
The good old thirties aren't so bad.
Life doesn't end at twenty-nine,
So come on in, the water's fine.
I, too, when thirty crossed my path,
Turned ugly colors with shame and wrath.
I kicked, I scratched, I bit my nails,
I indulged in tantrums the size of whales,
I found it hard to forgive my mater
For not having had me ten years later.
I struggled with reluctant feet
Where dotage and abdomens meet.
Like the tongue that seeks the missing tooth
I yearned for my extracted youth.
Since then some years have ambled by
And who so satisfied as I.
The thirties are things I wallow among,
With naught but pity for the young.
The less long ago that people were born
The more I gaze on them with scorn,
And each Thanksgiving I Thanksgive
That I'm slowly learning how to live.
So conquer, boy, your grief and rage,
And welcome to the perfect age!
I hope good fairies your footsteps haunt,
And bring you everything you want,
From cowboy suits and Boy Scout knives,
To beautiful, generous, wealthy wives.
If you play the horses, may you play good horses,
If you want divorces, may you get divorces,
Be it plenty of sleep, or fortune, or fame,
Or to carry the ball for Notre Dame,
Whatever it is you desire or covet,
My boy, I hope you get it and love it.
And you'll use it a great deal better, I know,
Than the child that you were a day ago.

# WHO UNDERSTANDS WHO ANYHOW?

There is one phase of life that I have never heard discussed
in any seminar,
And that is that all women think men are funny and all men
think that weminar.
Be the air the air of America or England or Japan,
It is full of husbands up in it saying, Isn't that just like a
woman? And wives saying, Isn't that just like a man?
Well, it so happens that this is a unique fight,
Because both sides are right.
Each sex keeps on laughing at the other sex for not thinking
the way they do,
Which is the cause of most domestic to-do and a-do,
Because breakfast is punctuated with spousely snorts,
Because husbands are jeering at their wives because they
ignore the front page and read society and fashions, and
wives are jeering at their husbands because they ignore
the front page and read finance and sports,
And men think that women have an easy time because all
they have to do is look after the household,
And what does that amount to but keeping an eye on the
children and seeing that three meals a day are served
and not allowing any litter to collect that would furnish
a foothold for a mousehold?
And women think that men have an easy time because all they
have to do is sit in an office all day long swapping stories
and scratching up desks with their heels,
And going out to restaurants and ordering everything they
like for their midday meals.
And oh yes, women like to resent the thought that they think
men think they are toys,
And men like to bask in the thought that they think women
think they are just big overgrown boys.
Well all these conflicting thoughts make for trouble at times
but on the whole it is a sound idea for men and women
to think different,
It is a topic upon which I am verbose and vociferant.
To it I dedicate my pen,

Because who would want to live in a world where the men
    all thought like women and the women all thought like
    men?
No, no, kind sirs, I will take all my hard-earned money,
And I will bet it on the nose of the tribe whose men and
    women continue to think each other are funny.

---

## COMPLAINT TO FOUR ANGELS

Every night at sleepy-time
Into bed I gladly climb.
Every night anew I hope
That with the covers I can cope.

Adjust the blanket fore and aft,
Swallow next a soothing draught;
Then a page of Scott or Cooper
May induce a healthful stupor.

O the soft luxurious darkness,
Fit for Morgan, or for Harkness!
Traffic dies along the street.
The light is out. So are your feet.

Adjust the blanket aft and fore,
Sigh, and settle down once more.
Behold, a breeze! The curtains puff.
One blanket isn't quite enough.

Yawn and rise and seek your slippers,
Which, by now, are cold as kippers.
Yawn, and stretch, and prod yourself,
And fetch a blanket from the shelf.

And so to bed again, again,
Cozy under blankets twain.
Welcome warmth and sweet nirvana
Till eight o'clock or so mañana.

You sleep as deep as Keats or Bacon;
Then you dream and toss and waken.
Where is the breeze? There isn't any.
Two blankets, boy, are one too many.

O stilly night, why are you not
Consistent in your cold and hot?
O slumber's chains, unlocked so oft
With blankets being donned or doffed!

The angels who should guard my bed
I fear are slumbering instead.
O angels, please resume your hovering;
I'll sleep, and you adjust the covering.

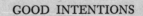

GOOD INTENTIONS

# YOU AND ME AND P. B. SHELLEY

What is life? Life is stepping down a step or sitting in a chair,
And it isn't there.
Life is not having been told that the man has just waxed the
   floor,
It is pulling doors marked PUSH and pushing doors marked
   PULL and not noticing notices which say PLEASE USE
   OTHER DOOR.
It is when you diagnose a sore throat as an unprepared
   geography lesson and send your child weeping to school
   only to be returned an hour later covered with spots that
   are indubitably genuine,
It is a concert with a trombone soloist filling in for Yehudi
   Menuhin.
Were it not for frustration and humiliation
I suppose the human race would get ideas above its station.
Somebody once described Shelley as a beautiful and in-
   effective angel beating his luminous wings against the
   void in vain,
Which is certainly describing with might and main,
But probably means that we are all brothers under our pelts,
And Shelley went around pulling doors marked PUSH and
   pushing doors marked PULL just like everybody else.

---

## GLOSSINA MORSITANS, OR, THE TSETSE

A *Glossina morsitans* bit rich Aunt Betsy.
Tsk tsk, tsetse.

## NOW TELL ME ABOUT YOURSELF

Everybody speaks of being patronized,

Yet nobody speaks of the truly irksome shambles which is, or are, being matronized,

By which I mean that there is nothing more impolitely and noticeably aloof

Than a woman of a certain sort sounding out a man of whose certain sort she hasn't yet got definite affidavits or proof.

She displays the great names of her acquaintance for his benefit like a *nouveau riche* displaying his riches.

And fixes him with the stare of a psychiatrist to see if there is one at which he twitches.

George Washington and George Sand and Lloyd George to her are Georgie,

And she would have addressed the Borgias behind their backs as Borgie.

She always wants to know, first, where do you come from, and second, do you of course know Babs and Bonzo Beaver there, which you never do, often for your own very good reasons, but you try to make your reply a polite one.

So you murmur, "Well I don't really know them, but I know *of* them," and she at once assigns you to your proper side of the tracks, and it is not the right one.

When she discusses national affairs she doesn't talk exactly treasonably.

But she refers to that part of the nation which lies outside of New York in the bright tone of one referring to a little tailor she has just discovered who does alterations very reasonably.

Please do not get the impression that a matronizing woman causes me to froth at the mouth or slaver;

I only wish to notify you that whenever you want her you can have her.

## TIN WEDDING WHISTLE

Though you know it anyhow
Listen to me, darling, now,

Proving what I need not prove
How I know I love you, love.

Near and far, near and far,
I am happy where you are;

Likewise I have never learnt
How to be it where you aren't.

Far and wide, far and wide,
I can walk with you beside;

Furthermore, I tell you what,
I sit and sulk where you are not.

Visitors remark my frown
When you're upstairs and I am down,

Yes, and I'm afraid I pout
When I'm indoors and you are out;

But how contentedly I view
Any room containing you.

In fact I care not where you be,
Just as long as it's with me.

In all your absences I glimpse
Fire and flood and trolls and imps.

Is your train a minute slothful?
I goad the stationmaster wrothful.

When with friends to bridge you drive
I never know if you're alive,

And when you linger late in shops
I long to telephone the cops.

Yet how worth the waiting for,
To see you coming through the door.

Somehow, I can be complacent
Never but with you adjacent.

Near and far, near and far,
I am happy where you are;

Likewise, I have never learnt
How to be it where you aren't.

Then grudge me not my fond endeavor,
To hold you in my sight forever;

Let none, not even you, disparage
Such valid reason for a marriage.

---

## APRIL YULE, DADDY!

Roses are things which Christmas is not a bed of them,
Because it is the day when parents finally realize that their
    children will always be a jump ahead of them.
You stay up all night trimming the tree into a veritable fairy-
    land and then in the joyous morn you spring it on the
    children in a blaze of glory, and who says Ooh!?
You.
And you frantically point out the dictator's ransom in build-

ing sets and bicycles and embarrassingly lifelike dolls
  with which the room is checkered,
And the little ones pay about as much attention to them as
  they would to the punctuation in the *Congressional
  Record,*
Because they are fully occupied in withdrawing all the books
  from the bookcase to build a house to house the pup in,
Or pulling down the curtains to dress up in,
And you stand hangdoggedly around because you haven't any
  place to go,
And after a while they look casually over at the dictator's
  ransom and say, "Are those the presents? Oh."
And you console yourself by thinking Ah happy apathy, as
  long as we haven't had an emotional climax maybe we
  won't have an emotional anticlimax, maybe we'll get
  through the day without hysterics, ah happy apathy,
Ah may this Yuletide indeed turn out to be Yuletide without
  mishapathy.
Ah could this sensational lull but be permanent instead of pro
  tem;
Ah and doubly ah, if Christmas day could but end at eleven
  A.M.!—
But it doesn't, but the lull does, and here's something else
  you discover as you keep on living,
Which is that Christmas doesn't end for about two weeks
  after Christmas, but it starts all over again right after the
  following Thanksgiving.

---

I'M SURE SHE SAID SIX-THIRTY

One of the hardest explanations to be found
Is an explanation for just standing around.
Anyone just standing around looks pretty sinister,
Even a minister;
Consider then the plight of the criminal,

Who lacks even the protective coloration of a hyminal,
And as just standing around is any good criminal's practically
daily stint,
I wish to proffer a hint.
Are you, sir, a masher who blushes as he loiters,
Do you stammer to passers-by that you are merely expecting
a street car, or a dispatch from Reuter's?
Or perhaps you are a safeblower engaged in casing a joint;
Can you look the patrolman in the eye or do you forget all the
*savoir-faire* you ever loint?
Suppose you are a shoplifter awaiting an opportunity to lift a
shop,
Or simply a novice with a length of lead pipe killing time in a
dark alley pending the arrival of a wealthy fop,
Well, should any official ask you why you are just standing
around,
Do you wish you could simply sink into the ground?
My dear sir, do not be embarrassed, do not reach for your
gun or your knife,
Remember the password, which, uttered in a tone of quiet
despair, is the explanation of anyone's standing around
anywhere at any hour for any length of time: "I'm waiting for my wife."

---

## WE DON'T NEED TO LEAVE YET, DO WE?
## OR, YES WE DO

One kind of person when catching a train always wants to
allow an hour to cover the ten-block trip to the terminus,
And the other kind looks at them as if they were verminous,
And the second kind says that five minutes is plenty and will
even leave one minute over for buying the tickets,
And the first kind looks at them as if they had cerebral rickets.
One kind when theater-bound sups lightly at six and hastens
off to the play,

And indeed I know one such person who is so such that it frequently arrives in time for the last act of the matinee,

And the other kind sits down at eight to a meal that is positively sumptuous,

Observing cynically that an eight-thirty curtain never rises till eight-forty, an observation which is less cynical than bumptuous.

And what the first kind, sitting uncomfortably in the waiting room while the train is made up in the yards, can never understand,

Is the injustice of the second kind's reaching their seat just as the trains moves out, just as they had planned,

And what the second kind cannot understand as they stumble over the first kind's feet just as the footlights flash on at last

Is that the first kind doesn't feel the least bit foolish at having entered the theater before the cast.

Oh, the first kind always wants to start now and the second kind always wants to tarry,

Which wouldn't make any difference, except that each other is what they always marry.

---

## THE SCREEN WITH THE FACE WITH THE VOICE

How long
Is a song?
O Lord,
How long?
A second?
A minute?
An hour?
A day?
A decade?
A cycle of Cathay?
Press the ears

With occlusive fingers;
The whining melody
Lingers, lingers;
The mouthing face
Will not be hid,
But leers at the eye
From the inner lid.
With the sure advance of ultimate doom
The moaning adenoids larger loom;
The seven-foot eyebrows fall and rise
In roguish rapture or sad surprise;
Eyeballs roll with fine emotion,
Like buoys rocked by a treacle ocean;
Tugged like the bell above the chapel,
Tosses the giant Adam's apple;
Oozes the voice from the magic screen,
A slow Niagara of Grenadine;
A frenzy of ripe orgiastic pain,
Niagara gurgling down a drain.

How long
Is a song?
O Lord,
How long?
As long as Loew,
And Keith,
And Albee;
It Was,
And Is,
And Always Shall Be.
This is the string Time may not sever,
This is the music that lasts forever,
This is the Womb,
This is the Tomb,
This is Alpha, Omega, and Oom!
The eyes, the eyes shall follow you!
The throat, the throat shall swallow you!
Hygienic teeth shall wolf you!
And viscous voice engulf you!

The lolloping tongue itself answer your question!
The Adam's Apple dance at your ingestion!
And you shall never die, but live to nourish the bowels
Of deathless celluloid vowels.

---

## I WANT A DRINK OF WATER, BUT NOT FROM THE THERMOS

Have you ever lost your early start on a six-hundred-mile trip
and had to spend the night in an individual wayside slum
instead of the cozy inn at which you had foresightedly
engaged rooms because child A couldn't find her abso-
lutely favorite doll, and when she did find it, child B
hadn't finished plaiting her hair yet?

Then you will agree with me that an accurate definition of a
millionth of a second is the interval between the moment when you press the starter as you begin a six-
hundred-mile trip and the moment when two little tired
voices inquire from the back seat, "Are we nearly there
yet?"

Then again, consider the other millionth of a second which
lasts a year, when Time stands still, and Eternity in the
lap of Infinity lingers,

Which is while you sit in helpless paralysis while child B
carefully slams the door on child A's fingers.

Take the battle royal whose results no bachelor need ever
have computed,

Which is the struggle to sit nearest to the open window, a
struggle the prize for which is the privilege of sticking
the head and arms out in just the right position to be
immediately amputated.

Yes, for the father of none to thank his stars I think it only
behooving,

If merely because he has not to contend with little ones who
will descend from the car only on the traffic side, and

[ 147 ]

preferably quite some time before the car but not the
  traffic has stopped moving.
Yes, he can roll along as confident as brass;
No restlessly whirling little leg will knock his spectacles off
  as he confronts a bus, no little hand groping the floor
  for a vanilla ice cream cone with chocolate thingamajigs
  on it will suddenly alight heavily upon the gas.
As the father of two there is a respectful question which I
  wish to ask of fathers of five:
How do you happen to be still alive?

---

## THE TROUBLE WITH WOMEN IS MEN

A husband is a man who two minutes after his head touches
  the pillow is snoring like an overloaded omnibus,
Particularly on those occasions when between the humidity
  and the mosquitoes your own bed is no longer a bed, but
  an insomnibus,
And if you turn on the light for a little reading he is sensitive to the faintest gleam,
But if by any chance you are asleep and he wakeful, he is not
  slow to rouse you with the complaint that he can't close
  his eyes, what about slipping downstairs and freezing
  him a cooling dish of pistachio ice cream.
His touch with a bottle opener is sure,
But he cannot help you get a tight dress over your head without catching three hooks and a button in your coiffure.
Nor can he so much as wash his ears without leaving an inch
  of water on the bathroom linoleum,
But if you mention it you evoke not a promise to splash no
  more but a mood of deep melancholium.
Indeed, each time he transgresses your chance of correcting
  his faults grows lesser,
Because he produces either a maddeningly logical explanation

[ 148 ]

or a look of martyrdom which leaves you instead of him
feeling the remorse of the transgressor.

Such are husbandly foibles, but there are moments when a
foible ceases to be a foible.

Next time you ask for a glass of water and when he brings it
you have a needle almost threaded and instead of set-
ting it down he stands there holding it out to you, just
kick him fairly hard in the stomach, you will find it
thoroughly enjoible.

---

### THE GANDER

Be careful not to cross the gander,
A bird composed of beak and dander.
His heart is filled with prideful hate
Of all the world except his mate,
And if the neighbors do not err
He's overfond of beating her.
Is she happy? What's the use
Of trying to psychoanalyze a goose?

---

### DANCE UNMACABRE

This is the witching hour of noon;
Bedlam breaks upon us soon.
When the stroke of twelve has tolled
What a pageant doth unfold.
Drawers slam on pads of notes,
Eager fingers clutch at coats;
Compact, lipstick, comb and hat,
Here a dab and there a pat;

The vital letter just begun
Can sulk in the machine till one.
Stenographers on clicking heels
Scurry forth in quest of meals;
Secretaries arm in arm
Fill the corridors with charm;
The stolid air with scent grows heavy
As bevy scuttles after bevy;
Like the pipers on the beach,
Calling shrilly each to each,
Sure as arrows, swift as skaters,
Converging at the elevators.
From the crowded lift they scatter
Bursting still with turbulent chatter;
The revolving door in rapture whirls
Its quarters full of pretty girls.
*Soignée, comme il faut* and *chic*
On forty or forty-five a week.
When One upon the dial looms
They hurry to their office tombs,
There to bide in dust till five,
When they come again alive.

---

## SUPPOSE HE THREW IT IN YOUR FACE

Please don't anybody ask me to decide anything, I do not
know a nut from a meg,
Or which came first, the lady or the tiger, or which came
next, the chicken or the egg.
I am, alas, to be reckoned
With the shortstop who can't decide whether to throw to
first or second,
Nor can I decide whether to put, except after c,
E before i, or i before e.
But where this twilight mind really goes into eclipse

Is in the matter of tips.
I stand stricken before the triple doom,
Whether, and How Much, and Whom.
Tell me, which is more unpleasant,
The look from him who is superior to a tip and gets it, or
    from him who isn't and doesn't?
I had rather be discovered playing with my toes in the
    Aquarium
Than decide wrongly about an honorarium.
Oh, to dwell forever amid Utopian scenery
Where hotels and restaurants and service stations are operated
    by untippable unoffendable machinery.

---

## SO THAT'S WHO I REMIND ME OF

When I consider men of golden talents,
I'm delighted, in my introverted way,
To discover, as I'm drawing up the balance,
How much we have in common, I and they.

Like Burns, I have a weakness for the bottle,
Like Shakespeare, little Latin and less Greek;
I bite my fingernails like Aristotle;
Like Thackeray, I have a snobbish streak.

I'm afflicted with the vanity of Byron,
I've inherited the spitefulness of Pope;
Like Petrarch, I'm a sucker for a siren,
Like Milton, I've a tendency to mope.

My spelling is suggestive of a Chaucer;
Like Johnson, well, I do not wish to die
(I also drink my coffee from the saucer);
And if Goldsmith was a parrot, so am I.

Like Villon, I have debits by the carload,
Like Swinburne, I'm afraid I need a nurse;
By my dicing is Christopher out-Marlowed,
And I dream as much as Coleridge, only worse.

In comparison with men of golden talents,
I am all a man of talent ought to be;
I resemble every genius in his vice, however henious—
Yet I only write like me.

---

## DR. FELL AND POINTS WEST

Your train leaves at eleven-forty-five and it is now but eleven-
     thirty-nine and a half,
And there is only one man ahead of you at the ticket window
     so you have plenty of time, haven't you, well I hope
     you enjoy a hearty laugh,
Because he is Dr. Fell, and he is engaged in an intricate
     maneuver,
He wants to go to Sioux City with stopovers at Plymouth
     Rock, Stone Mountain, Yellowstone Park, Lake Louise
     and Vancouver,
And he would like some information about an alternate route,
One that would include New Orleans and Detroit, with possi-
     bly a day or two in Minneapolis and Butte,
And when the agent has compiled the data with the aid of a
     slug of aromatic spirits and a moist bandanna,
He says that settles it, he'll spend his vacation canoeing up
     and down the Susquehanna,
And oh yes, which way is the bus terminal and what's playing
     at the Rivoli,
And how do the railroads expect to stay in business when
     their employees are incapable of answering a simple
     question accurately or civilly?
He then demands and receives change for twenty dollars and
     saunters off leaving everybody's jaw with a sag on it,

And when you finally get to buy your ticket not only has your
train gone but you also discover that your porter has
efficiently managed to get your bag on it.

---

## THOUGHTS THOUGHT ON AN AVENUE

There would be far less masculine gaming and boozing
But for the feminine approach to feminine fashions, which is
distinctly confusing.
Please correct me if, although I don't think I do, I err;
But it is a fact that a lady wants to be dressed exactly like
everybody else but she gets pretty upset if she sees any-
body else dressed exactly like her.
Nothing so infuriates her as a similar hat or dress,
Especially if bought for less,
Which brings up another point which I will attempt to dis-
cuss in my guttural masculine jargon;
Her ideal raiment is costlier than her or her dearest friend's
purse can buy, and at the same time her own exclusive
and amazing bargain.
Psychologists claim that men are the dreamers and women
are the realists,
But to my mind women are the starriest-eyed of idealists,
Though I am willing to withdraw this charge and gladly eat
it uncomplaineously
If anyone can explain to me how a person can wear a costume
that is different from other people's and the same as other
people's, and more expensive than other people's and
cheaper than other people's, simultaneously.

# THOUGHTS THOUGHT WHILE WAITING FOR A PRONOUNCEMENT FROM A DOCTOR, AN EDITOR, A BIG EXECUTIVE, THE DEPARTMENT OF INTERNAL REVENUE OR ANY OTHER MOMENTOUS PRONOUNCER

Is Time on my hands? Yes it is, it is on my hands and my face
    and my torso and my tendons of Achilles,
And frankly, it gives me the willies.
The quarter-hour grows to the half-hour as chime clings to
    the tail of the preceding chime,
And I am tarred and feathered with Time.
No matter how frantically I shake my hands the hours will not
    drop off or evaporate,
Nor will even the once insignificant minutes co-operate.
The clock has stopped at Now, there is no Past, no Future,
    and oddly enough also no Now,
Only the hot, moist, beaded seconds on the brow,
Only the days and nights in a gluey lump,
And the smothering weeks that stick like a swarm of bees to a
    stump.
Times stands still, or it moves forward or backward, or at
    least it exists, for Ex-Senator Rush Holt, for Doctor
    Dafoe, for Simon and Schuster, yes, and for Schiaparelli,
But for me it is limbo akimbo, an inverted void, a mouse with
    its tail pulled out of its mouth through its belly.
O, the world's most honored watch, I haven't been there, I've
    been here,
For how long, for one small seventeen-jeweled tick, or have
    I been sitting a year?
I'm a speck in infinite space,
Entombed behind my face.
Shall I suddenly start to gyrate, to rotate, to spiral, to expand
    through nebular process to a new universe maybe, or
    maybe only a galaxy?
But such a Goldbergian scheme to extinguish one lonely
    identity seems, well, undersimplified and, if I may say so,
    smart-alexy.

Oh, I shall arise and go now, preferably in a purple-and-gold
 palanquin,
Borne on the copper shoulders of a Seminole, an Apache, a
 Crow and an Algonquin,
And whatever be my heart's desire, be it a new understanding of Time or a cup of dew gathered from the spring's
 first jonquil,
Why if none of the other three will bring it to me, why perhaps the Algonquil.

---

## SAMSON AGONISTES

I test my bath before I sit,
And I'm always moved to wonderment
That what chills the finger not a bit
Is so frigid upon the fundament.

---

## SEEING EYE TO EYE IS BELIEVING

When speaking of people and their beliefs I wear my belief
 on my sleeve;
I believe that people believe what they believe they believe.
When people reject a truth or an untruth it is not because it
 is a truth or an untruth that they reject it,
No, if it isn't in accord with their beliefs in the first place
 they simply say, "Nothing doing," and refuse to inspect
 it.
Likewise when they embrace a truth or an untruth it is not
 for either its truth or its mendacity,
But simply because they have believed it all along and there-

fore regard the embrace as a tribute to their own fair-
mindedness and sagacity.

These are enlightened days in which you can get hot water
and cold water out of the same spigot,

And everybody has something about which they are proud to
be broad-minded but they also have other things about
which you would be wasting your breath if you tried to
convince them that they were a bigot,

And I have no desire to get ugly,

But I cannot help mentioning that the door of a bigoted mind
opens outwards so that the only result of the pressure of
facts upon it is to close it more snugly.

Naturally I am not pointing a finger at me,

But I must admit that I find any speaker far more convinc-
ing when I agree with him than when I disagree.

---

### THE STRANGE CASE OF MR. NIOBOB'S TRANSMOGRIFICATION

Listen motorists, and learn:

Once there was a motorist named Mr. Niobob who took a trip
from which he didn't return.

His first five miles were simply seraphic

Because he was on a dual highway and there wasn't even a
smattering of traffic

But then he had to leave the dual highway because his destination was merely New York,

And dual highways never go to anybody's destination, they all
lead to a deserted traffic circle in Yoakum Corners or
Medicine Fork,

So Mr. Niobob turned off the trafficless dual highway and
with his usual luck,

Well yes, he immediately found himself behind a truck,

And whenever to pass it he mustered his nerve

Well, naturally, they came to a curve,

[ 156 ]

And it also bored him
That whenever the road straightened out and he edged over
    for a dash there would be another truck clattering to-
    ward him,
And he wished he had picked up a little voodoo on his cruise
    to Haiti,
Because while the truck bogged down to three miles per hour
    on the way uphill, why when he thought to overtake it
    on the way down it accelerated to eighty,
And all of a sudden they again entered a dual highway,
And Mr. Niobob said, "By gum, now I can drive my way,"
And he stepped on the gas with all his might,
And just as he overtook the truck it turned down a side road
    on the right.
Poor frustrated Mr. Niobob, his mind slipped quietly over
    the brink,
He just sat down and cried and cried until a kind Com-
    missioner of Motor Vehicles took pity on him and trans-
    formed him into a fountain, at which tired truck drivers
    often pause to drink.

---

## AND THREE HUNDRED AND SIXTY-SIX
## IN LEAP YEAR

Some people shave before bathing,
And about people who bathe before shaving they are scathing,
While those who bathe before shaving,
Well, they imply that those who shave before bathing are
    misbehaving.
Suppose you shave before bathing, well the advantage is that
    you don't have to make a special job of washing the
    lather off afterwards, it just floats off with the rest of
    your accumulations in the tub,
But the disadvantage is that before bathing your skin is hard

and dry and your beard confronts the razor like a grizzly
bear defending its cub.
Well then, suppose you bathe before shaving, well the advantage is that after bathing your skin is soft and moist,
and your beard positively begs for the blade,
But the disadvantage is that to get the lather off you have to
wash your face all over again at the basin almost immediately after washing it in the tub, which is a duplication
of effort that leaves me spotless but dismayed.
The referee reports, gentlemen, that Fate has loaded the dice,
Since your only choice is between walking around all day
with a sore chin or washing your face twice.

---

## FRAILTY, THY NAME IS A MISNOMER

Once there was a couple named Mr. and Mrs. Pepperloaf
and they were simply devoted,
Because each other was upon what they doted,
And in Mrs. Pepperloaf's eyes Mr. Pepperloaf could never err,
And he admitted only one flaw in her,
But it was a flaw which took many virtues to assuage,
Consisting in always asking him the date while she was read-
ing the paper with the date clearly printed on every
page,
And whenever he called her attention to this least admirable
of her traits
She would retort that he didn't trust the paper's weather
forecasts so then why should she trust its dates.
For eleven years his patience held
But finally he rebelled.
It was on the evening of Friday the seventh that she looked
up from her paper and asked him the date,
And he replied firmly that she would find it at the top of the
page so she looked at the top of the page and that was
that, and presently they sat down to supper and ate,

[ 158 ]

And they were miserable because they had never disagreed
    and this contretemps was a beginner for them,
And at nine his employer's wife called up to ask where were
    they, she and eleven guests were waiting dinner for them,
And Mr. Pepperloaf asked Mrs. Pepperloaf how she could
    have so misreckoned,
And she said she knew that they had been invited out on the
    seventh but, according to the newspaper he had in-
    structed her to consult, tonight was only the second,
And he picked up the paper and it was last week's, not
    today's,
And she said certainly, she had just been reading over some
    recipes for different delicious soufflés,
And now she found the first flaw in him because she had
    obeyed his order to look for the date in the paper, hadn't
    she, so his irritation was uncalled for and unseasonable.
Women would rather be right than reasonable.

---

## CELERY

Celery, raw,
Develops the jaw,
But celery, stewed,
Is more quietly chewed.

---

## THE PARSNIP

The parsnip, children, I repeat,
Is simply an anemic beet.
Some people call the parsnip edible;
Myself, I find this claim incredible.

# I BURN MONEY

The song about the happy-go-lucky fellow who hasn't time
    to be a millionaire strikes me as pretty funny,
Because I am pretty happy-go-lucky myself but it isn't lack
    of time that keeps me from being a millionaire, it's lack
    of money,
But if anybody has a million that they're through with it,
Well, I know what I'd like to do with it.
My first acquisition would not be a lot of Old Masters or first
    editions or palatial palaces,
No, it would be to supply each of my pairs of pants with its
    own set of galluses.
I can also think of another extravagance with which to startle
    all beholders
Which is an attendant with no other duties than to apply
    antisunburn lotion to that vulnerable spot you can't get
    at yourself either by reaching over or under your shoul-
    ders.
Likewise I have an idea which should earn the gratitude of
    every regular-dinner eater alive,
Which is to promote a regular-dinner that when you order
    oysters or clams on it you get six oysters or clams instead
    of five.
My next goal is one to reach which I should probably have
    to sink into debt,
But it would be worth it because it is the development of a
    short, hot, harsh, quick-burning, full-of-nicotine cigarette.
A million dollars could also be well spent in hiring somebody
    to invent some better rhymes for wife than rife and knife
    and strife,
But I think what I would really do if I had a million would
    be to buy a millions dollars' worth of books written by
    me and then besides having a lot of good books I could
    sit back and live on the royalties for the rest of my life.

## THE CANTALOUPE

One cantaloupe is ripe and lush,
Another's green, another's mush.
I'd buy a lot more cantaloupe
If I possessed a fluoroscope.

---

## THE OCTOPUS

Tell me, O Octopus, I begs,
Is those things arms, or is they legs?
I marvel at thee, Octopus;
If I were thou, I'd call me Us.

---

## A BULLETIN HAS JUST COME IN

The rabbit's dreamy eyes grow dreamier
As he quietly gives you tularemia.

The parrot clashes his hooked proboscis
And laughs while handing you psittacosis.

In every swamp or wooded area
Mosquito witches brew malaria.

We risk at every jolly picnic
Spotted fever from a tick nick.

People perish of bubonic;
To rats, it's better than a tonic.

The hog converted into pork
Puts trichinosis on your fork.

The dog today that guards your babies
Tomorrow turns and gives them rabies.

The baby, once all milk and spittle,
Grows to a Hitler, and boy, can he hittle!

That's our planet, and we're stuck with it.
I wish its inheritors the best of luck with it.

---

## THE EEL

I don't mind eels
Except as meals.

---

## THE WASP

The wasp and all his numerous family
I look upon as a major calamily.
He throws open his nest with prodigality,
But I distrust his waspitality.

---

## NOT GEORGE WASHINGTON'S, NOT ABRAHAM LINCOLN'S, BUT MINE

Well, here I am thirty-eight,
Well, I certainly thought I'd have longer to wait.
You just stop in for a couple of beers,
And gosh, there go thirty-seven years.

Well, it has certainly been fun,
But I certainly thought I'd have got a lot more done.
Why if I had been really waked up and alive,
I could have been a Congressman since I was twenty-one or President since I was thirty-five.
I guess I know the reason my accomplishments are so measly:
I don't comprehend very easily.
It finally dawned on me that in life's race I was off to a delayed start
When at the age of thirty-three I had to be told that I could swim faster if I'd keep my fingers together instead of spreading them apart,
And I was convinced that precociousness was not the chief of my faults
When it was only last winter that I discovered that the name of that waltz that skaters waltz to is "The Skaters' Waltz."
After thirty-seven years I find myself the kind of man that anybody can sell anything to,
And nobody will ever tell anything to.
Whenever people get up a party of which I am to be a member to see some picture which I don't want to see because I am uninterested in the situation that Scarlett and Mr. Chips are estranged over,
Why my head is what it is arranged over.
Contrariwise, I myself not only can't sell anybody anything,
I can't even ever tell anybody anything.
I have never yet had a good gossip bomb all poised and ready to burst
That somebody hasn't already told everybody first.
Yes, my career to date has certainly been a fiasco;
It would not have made a thrilling dramatic production for the late Oliver Morosco or the late David Belasco.
But in spite of the fact that my career has been a fiasco to date,
Why I am very proud and happy to be thirty-eight.

## THE KANGAROO

O Kangaroo, O Kangaroo,
Be grateful that you're in the zoo,
And not transmuted by a boomerang
To zestful tangy Kangaroo meringue.

---

## DON'T WAIT, HIT ME NOW!

If there are any wives present who wish to irritate their hus-
    bands or husbands who wish to irritate their wives,
Why I know an irritation more irritating than hives,
So if you think such an irritation expedient,
Here is the formula, in which the presence of a third person
    is the only essential extra ingredient;
Indeed is it beautifully simple,
But it is guaranteed to make a molehill out of a dimple
And what it consists of is that when you are annoyed with
    your husband or wife and want to do the opposite of woo
    them,
Why, you just talk at them instead of to them.
Suppose you think your Gregory danced too often with Mrs.
    Limbworthy at the club, you don't say to him directly,
    "Gregory I'll smack you down if you don't lay off that
    platinum-plated hussy,"
No, you wait till a friend drops in and then with a glance at
    Gregory say to her, "Isn't it funny what fools middle-aged
    men can make of themselves over anything blonde and
    slithery, do you understand how anybody sober and in
    their right mind could look twice at that Limbworthy
    job, but then of course darling, Gregory wasn't alto-
    gether in his right mind last night, was he?"
This is indeed more excruciating to Gregory than Shakes-
    pearean excursion and alarums,
Because there is no defense agains caroms.

Or let us suppose you are irked by your Esmeralda's sudden passion for antiques.

Well you don't mention it for weeks,

No, you wait till a friend drops in and then with a glance at Esmeralda you say, "How anybody can be sucked in by this antique racket is beyond me, but there are some otherwise sensible women who'll mortgage their beauty treatments for a genuine early American paper doily or a guaranteed second-hand Killarney banshee,

But of course Esmeralda can't ever resist an opportunity to pick up some fossil to amaze her friends with, can she?"

And Esmeralda must sit quiet and take it with apparent docility,

Because the hit direct doesn't compare with the richochet in deadly unanswerability.

By this easy method can every Gregory score off every Esmeralda and every Esmeralda annihilate every Gregory,

And its only drawback besides eventual divorce is that it reduces all their friends to emotional beggary.

---

## I'LL WRITE THEIR NUMBER DOWN WHEN WE GET HOME

Words, idle words, are what people's social life contains a goodly store of,

And the idlest words are contained in the wishful phrase beginning, Why don't we see more of?

By the time your age is medium,

Well, your most exotic evenings are placid to the point of tedium,

Because whenever you step out you find yourself stepping out amid faces and ideas that are, to say the least, familiar,

Which is a situation which moves only from the willy-nilly to the willy-nillier,

But once in every eleven blue moons you encounter a new-
    comer in your little coterie,
And it doesn't matter whether he is a veteran or a veterinary
    or a vestryman or a vegetarian or a notable or a
    Notogæan or a notary,
Because his fresh point of view is as beneficial to anemic
    conversation as a transfusion or a tonic,
And his wife is equally attractive and stimulating, and the
    future would be cute as a button if it weren't so in-
    evitably ironic,
Because on the way home you say "My I like those people,
    why don't we see more of them?" and it is agreed that
    Yes we certainly must, and from then on they might as
    well be living in the ancient Anglian kingdom of Mercia,
Because you never see them again because you never do any-
    thing about it except to murmur "Why don't we see more
    of them?" and that is why the best definition I can think
    of for at least one man's social life is simply inertia.

---

## THE FLY

God in His wisdom made the fly
And then forgot to tell us why.

---

## ASK DADDY, HE WON'T KNOW

Now that they've abolished chrome work
I'd like to call their attention to home work.
Here it is only three decades since my scholarship was
    famous,
And I'm an ignoramus.

I cannot think which goes sideways and which goes up and
     down, a parallel or a meridian,
Nor do I know the name of him who first translated the Bible
     into Indian, I see him only as an enterprising colonial
     Gideon.
I have difficulty with dates,
To say nothing of the annual rainfall of the Southern Central
     States.
Naturally the correct answers are just back of the tip of my
     tongue,
But try to explain that to your young.
I am overwhelmed by their erudite banter,
I am in no condition to differentiate between Tamerlane and
     Tam o' Shanter.
I reel, I sway, I am utterly exhausted;
Should you ask me when Chicago was founded I could only
     reply I didn't even know it was losted.

---

## THE TERMITE

Some primal termite knocked on wood
And tasted it, and found it good,
And that is why your Cousin May
Fell through the parlor floor today.

YOU CAN'T GET THERE FROM HERE

## AND HOW KEEN WAS
## THE VISION OF SIR LAUNFAL?

Man's earliest pastime, I suppose,
Was to play with his fingers and his toes.
Then later, wearying of himself,
He devised the monster and the elf,
Enlivening his existence drab
With Blunderbore and Puck and Mab.
A modern man, in modern Maryland,
I boast my private gate to fairyland,
My kaleidoscope, my cornucopia,
My own philosopher's stone, myopia.
Except when rationalized by lenses,
My world is not what other men's is;
Unless I have my glasses on,
The postman is a leprechaun,
I can wish on either of two new moons,
Billboards are graven with mystic runes,
Shirts hung to dry are ragtag gypsies,
Mud puddles loom like Mississipsies,
And billiard balls resemble plums,
And street lamps are chrysanthemums.
If my vision were twenty-twenty,
I should miss miracles aplenty.

---

## OAFISHNESS SELLS GOOD, LIKE AN
## ADVERTISEMENT SHOULD

I guess it is farewell to grammatical compunction,
I guess a preposition is the same as a conjunction,
I guess an adjective is the same as an adverb,
And "to parse" is a bad verb.
Blow, blow, thou winter wind,
Thou are not that unkind

Like man's ingratitude to his ancestors who left him the Eng-
lish language for an inheritance;
This is a chromium world in which even the Copley Plazas
and the Blackstones and the Book Cadillacs are simplified
into Sheratons.
I guess our ancient speech has gone so flat that we have to
spike it;
Like the hart panteth for the water brooks I pant for a re-
vival of Shakespeare's *Like You Like It*.
I can see the tense draftees relax and purr
When the sergeant barks, "Like you were."
—And don't try to tell me that our well has been defiled by
immigration;
Like goes Madison Avenue, like so goes the nation.

---

## RING OUT THE OLD, RING IN THE NEW, BUT DON'T GET CAUGHT IN BETWEEN

### 1. FIRST CHIME

If there is anything of which American industry has a super-
fluity
It is green lights, know-how, initiative and ingenuity.
If there is one maxim to American industry unknown
It is, Let well enough alone.
Some people award American industry an encomium
Because it not only paints the lily, it turns it into a two-toned
job with a forward look and backward fins and a calyx
trimmed with chromium.
I don't propose to engage in a series of Lincoln-Douglas de-
bates,
But take the matter of paper plates.
The future of many a marriage would have been in doubt
But for paper plates, which have imparted tolerability to
picnics and the maid's day out,

But the last paper plates I handled had been improved into
   plastic and they are so artistic that I couldn't throw
   them away,
And I ended up by washing them against another day.
Look at the automotive industry, how it never relaxes;
It has improved the low-priced three so much that instead of
   a thousand dollars they now cost twenty-nine seventy-
   five, not including federal and local taxes.
Do you know what I think?
Ordinary mousetraps will soon be so improved that they will
   be too good for the mice, who will be elbowed out by
   mink.

## 2. SECOND CHIME

That low keening you hear is me bemoaning my fate;
I am out of joint, I was born either too early or too late.
As the boll said to the weevil,
Get yourself born before the beginning or after the end, but
   never in the middle of, a technological upheaval.
I am adrift, but know not whether I am drifting seaward or
   shoreward,
My neck is stiff from my head trying to turn simultaneously
   backward and forward.
One way I know I am adrift,
My left foot keeps reaching for the clutch when the car has
   an automatic shift.
Another way that I am adrift I know,
I'm in a car that I've forgotten has a clutch and I stall it when
   the light says STOP and again when the light says Go.
I find that when dressing I behave as one being stung by
   gallinippers
Because half my trousers are old style and half new and I am
   forever zipping buttons and buttoning zippers.
I can no longer enjoy butter on my bread;
Radio and TV have taught me to think of butter as "You
   know what" or "The more expensive spread."
I am on the thin ice of the old order while it melts;

I guess that perhaps in this changing world money changes
    less than anything else.
That is one reason money is to me so dear;
I know I can't take it with me, I just want the use of some
    while I am here.

---

## PERIOD PERIOD

### PERIOD I

Our fathers claimed, by obvious madness moved,
Man's innocent until his guilt is proved.
They would have known, had they not been confused,
He's innocent until he is accused.

### PERIOD II

The catch phrase "Nothing human to me is alien"
Was coined by some South European rapscallion.
This dangerous fallacy I shall now illumine:
To committees, nothing alien is human.

---

## I SPY
### or
## THE DEPRAVITY OF PRIVACY

My voice is a minor one, but I must raise it;
I come not only to bury privacy, but to praise it.
Yes, this is my long farewell to privacy;
Democracy seems to have turned into a sort of Lady Go-
    divacy.
We are living in an era by publicity bewitched,

Where the Peeping Toms are not blinded, but enriched.
Keyhole-itis is contagious, and I fear that by our invasion of
the privacy of the people who clamor for their privacy
to be invaded,
Well, we are ourselves degraded;
And now that we can't leave the privacy of public personali-
ties alone
We end up by invading our own.
What puts a neighbor's teeth on edge?
Your growing a hedge.
He is irked because he can't see what you're doing on your
own lawn, raising tulips,
Or swigging juleps,
And curiosity is what he is in his knees up to,
And also exhibitionism, because he not only wants to know
what *you* are doing, he wants you to know what *he's*
up to,
So he has a picture window to look out through that he never
lowers the blinds on, so you can't help looking in through
it,
And you are forced to observe the nocturnal habits of him
and his kin through it.
Things have reached a pretty pass; even my two goldfish,
Jael and Sisera,
Complain that they have no more privacy than a candidate's
viscera.
Well, privacy is a wall,
And something there is that does not love it: namely, the
Pry family, Pauline and Paul.

# ANYBODY FOR MONEY?
## or
## JUST BRING YOUR OWN BASKET

Consider the banker.
He was once a financial anchor.
To pinch our pennies he would constantly implore us,
And if we wouldn't pinch them ourselves, he would pinch
   them for us.
Down to thrift he was always admonishing us to buckle,
Reminding us that many a mickle makes a muckle.
When with clients he was closeted,
He was attempting to convince them that everything ought
   to be made do, worn out, eaten up, or deposited.
In a word, if you wanted to catch up with the Joneses or bust,
You couldn't do either with the connivance of the First Na-
   tional Pablum Exchange & Trust.
Yes, bankers used to be like Scrooge before he encountered
   the ghost of Marley,
But along came TV and now they are Good-Time Charlie.
The jingle of coins multiplying at two per cent per annum
   has given way to the jingle of the singing commercial,
And their advertisements, implying that anyone who doesn't
   turn in his this year's car for a next year's model with
   all the latest excessories and borrow the difference from
   them is a frugal old fogy, range from the supplicatory
   to the coercial.
The way some people sing whiskily,
Bankers are singing fiscally.
Everything is hey-nonny-nonny,
Come in and get some money.
That bankers have only themselves to blame for the recent
   wave of holdups and embezzlements I think highly
   probable,
They are behaving so provocatively robbable.

# FEE FI HO HUM,
## NO WONDER BABY SUCKS HER THUMB

I don't know whether you know what's new in juvenile literature or not,

But I'll tell you what's new in juvenile literature, there's a
new plot.

I grew up on the old plot, which I considered highly satis-
factory,

And the hope of having stories containing it read to me re-
strained me occasionally from being mendacious or re-
fractory.

There were always two older sons and a youngest son, or two
older daughters and a youngest daughter,

And the older pair were always arrogant, selfish rascals, and
the youngest was always a numskull of the first water,

And the older ones would never share their bread and cheese
with little old men and women, and wouldn't help them
home with their loads,

And ended up with their fingers caught in cleft logs, or their
conversation issuing in the form of toads,

And the young numskulls never cared what happened to
their siblings, because they had no family loyalty,

They just turned over all their bread and cheese to elderly
eccentrics and ended up married to royalty, which I
suppose explains what eventually happened to royalty.

That was admittedly not a plot to strain the childish understanding,

But it was veritably Proustian compared to the new plot that
the third generation is demanding.

Whence these haggard looks?

I am trapped between one lovable grandchild and her two
detestable favorite books.

The first is about a little boy who lost his cap and looked
everywhere for it, behind the armchair and inside the re-
frigerator and under the bed,

And where do you think he found it? On his head!

The second is about a little girl who lost one shoe on the

train, and until she found it she would give the porter
and the other passengers no peace,
And finally where do you think she found it? In her valise!
A forthcoming book utilizing this new plot will tell the story
of a child who lost her grandfather while he was reading to her, and you'll never guess where she discovered
*him*.
Spang in the middle of Hans Christian Andersen and the
Brothers Grimm.

-------

## YOUR LEAD, PARTNER, I HOPE
## WE'VE READ THE SAME BOOK

When I was just a youngster,
Hardly bigger than a midge,
I used to join my family
In a game of auction bridge.
We were patient with reneging,
For the light was gas or oil,
And our arguments were settled
By a reference to Hoyle.
Auction bridge was clover;
Then the experts took it over.
You could no longer bid by the seat of your pants,
The experts substituted skill for chance.

The experts captured auction
With their lessons and their books,
And the casual week-end player
Got a lot of nasty looks.
The experts captured auction
And dissected it, and then
Somebody thought up contract,
And we played for fun again.
It was pleasant, lose or win,

But the experts muscled in,
And you couldn't deal cards in your own abode
Without having memorized the latest code.

We turned to simpler pastimes
With our neighbors and our kin;
Oklahoma or canasta,
Or a modest hand of gin.
We were quietly diverted
Before and after meals,
Till the experts scented suckers
And came yapping at our heels.
Behold a conquered province;
I'm a worm, and they are robins.
On the grandchildren's table what books are displayed?
*Better Slapjack,* and *How to Win at Old Maid.*

In a frantic final effort
To frivol expert-free,
I've invented Amaturo
For just my friends and me.
The deck has seven morkels
Of eleven guzzards each,
The game runs counterclockwise,
With an extra kleg for dreech,
And if you're caught with a gruice,
The score reverts to deuce.
I'll bet that before my cuff links are on the bureau
Some expert will have written *A Guide to Amaturo.*

## ANYBODY ELSE HATE NICKYNAMES?

These are the times when all our feminine notables are beau-
    tified
And, unfortunately, the times when all our masculine notables
    are cutified.
This is the day of public diminutives,
Of Virginny instead of Virginiatives.
You don't remember Addison Sims of Seattle, you remember
    Addie,
Who today drives a Caddie.
Today we are much togetherer than we were,
And Jerry is hurt unless you call him Jer.
Honest Jack disappears, and Jackies turn up like bad pennies,
And Lennies and Kennies.
*O tempora! O mores!* Or rather, O tempy, O mory!
O Binnorie, O Binnorie!
O idols with mouths of babes and feet of straw!
O shades of Jackie L. Sullivan and Jackie J. McGraw!
This infantilism has almost knocked me flat,
But I'm still fighting like a one-eyed Kilkenneth cat.

---

## THE SNARK WAS A BOOJUM WAS A PRAWN

A giant new prawn has been dredged up near Santiago, Chile . . .
it is succulent and mysterious. . . . The new prawn has not been
named, a fact that is causing no concern in Chile.—TIMES

Could some descending escalator
Deposit me below the equator,
I'd hunt me a quiet Chilean haunt,
Some Santiago restaurant;
The fact I speak no *Español*
Would handicap me not at all,
Since any language would be aimless

In ordering a tidbit nameless;
I'd simply tie my napkin on
And gesture like a giant prawn,
Then, served the dish for which I yearned,
Proceed to munch it, unconcerned.
Happy crustacean, anonymous prawn,
From distant Latin waters drawn,
Hadst thou in Yankee seas appeared,
Account executives would have cheered,
Vice-presidents in paroxysms
Accorded thee multiple baptisms;
Yea, shouldst thou hit our markets now,
Soon, prawn, wouldst thou be named—and how!
I see the bright ideas drawn:
Prawno, Prawnex, and Vitaprawn;
And, should upper-bracket dreamers wake,
Squab o' Neptune, and Plankton Steak.
Small wonder thou headest for Santiago,
Where gourmets ignore such frantic farrago;
That's exactly where I myself would have went if I'd
Been mysterious, succulent, unidentified.

---

## TRY IT SUNS. AND HOLS.; IT'S CLOSED THEN

I know a little restaurant
Behind a brownstone stoop
Where *potage du jour* is French
For a can of onion soup.

You order a Martini without an olive in it;
They bring you a Martini, it has an olive in it.
Throw the olive on the floor,
That's what the floor is for.

The tables teem with ladies
Tuned up by Mistress Arden,
And Muzak fills the air
With "In a Persian Garden."

You order legs of frog, and please omit the garlic;
They bring you legs of frog, all redolent of garlic.
Throw the frogs' legs on the floor,
That's what the floor is for.

The Daiquiris are flowing
Before the meal and after;
The smoke from fifty filter tips
Is shaken by the Schraffter.

You ask them for an ash tray, a receptacle for ashes;
They do not bring an ash tray, instead they bring a menu.
Throw the ashes on the floor,
That's what the floor is for.

I know a little restaurant
Where client and agent grapple,
Where *ananas au kirsch*
Is French for canned pineapple.

You ask them for the check, for *l'addition*, for the bill;
They do not bring the check, they bring another menu.
Throw the menu on the floor.
Walk quickly through the door,
That's what the door is for.

# WHAT, NO SHEEP?

WHAT, NO SHEEP? These are a few of the 600 products sold in the "sleep shop" of a New York department store.
*—From an advertisement of the*
*Consolidated Edison Company in the* TIMES

I don't need no sleepin' medicine—
I seen a ad by ole Con Edison.
Now when I lay me on my mattress
You kin hear me snore from hell to Hatteras,
With muh Sleep Record,
Muh Vaporizer,
Muh Electric Slippers,
Muh Yawn Plaque,
Muh Slumber Buzzer,
Muh miniature Electric Organ,
An' muh wonderful Electric Blanket.

My old woman couldn't eat her hominy—
Too wore out from the durned insominy.
She give insominy quite a larrupin',
Sleeps like a hibernatin' tarrapin,
With her Eye Shade,
Her Clock-Radio,
Her Sinus Mask,
Her Massagin' Pillow,
Her Snore Ball,
Her miniature Electric Organ,
An' her wonderful Electric Blanket.

Evenin's when the sunlight westers
I pity muh pioneer an-cestors.
They rode the wilderness wide and high,
But how did they ever go sleepy-bye
Without their Eye Shade,
Their Clock-Radio,
Their Sleep Record,
Their Vaporizer,

Their Sinus Mask,
Their Electric Slippers,
Their Yawn Plaque,
Their Slumber Buzzer,
Their Massagin' Pillow,
Their Snore Ball,
Their miniature Electric Organ,
An' their wonderful Electric Blanket?

---

## HO, VARLET! MY TWO CENTS' WORTH OF PENNY POSTCARD!

One thing about the past,
It is likely to last.
Some of it is horrid and some sublime,
And there is more of it all the time.
I happen to be one who dotes
On ruins and moats;
I like to think on the days when knights were bold and ladies demure,
And I regret that my strength is only as the strength of nine because my heart is not one hundred per cent pure.
However, I also like to think on periods other than the Arthurian,
I like to think on the period when most types of invertebrate marine life flourished and coral-reef building began— namely, the Silurian.
I believe that Cro-Magnon caves and huts on stilts in lakes would make nifty abodes,
And I am given to backward glances o'er traveled roads.
Because I am one in whom Waverley romanticism prevails,
I guess that is why I am fascinated by the United States mails.
The attitude of the Post Office Department is much to my taste;
It holds that posthaste makes post waste.

[ 184 ]

In these drab days when trains and airplanes fill the grade
    crossings and skies by the million,
The mails are still carried by dusty couriers on fat palfreys,
    riding pillion.
So as a dreamy-eyed antiquarian I hereby, dear Post Office
    Department, express my appreciation to you:
Thanks to whom we can diurnally eat archaic and have it, too.

---

## CAESAR KNIFED AGAIN
or
## CULTURE BIZ GETS HEP, BOFFS PROFS

To win the battle of life you have to plan strategical as well
    as tactical,
So I am glad that our colleges are finally getting practical.
If they're going to teach know-how
It's up to them to show how,
And one way to show it
Is to get rid of dead languages taught by professors who are
    also dead but don't know enough to know it.
It's high time to rescue our kids from poetry and prunes and
    prisms;
Once they start in on ideas and ideals they'll end up spout-
    ing ideologies and isms.
Get them interested in hotel management and phys. ed. and
    business administration instead of the so-called finer arts
And you'll cut off the flow of eggheads and do-gooders and
    bleeding hearts.
Every campus gets what it deserves and deserves what it gets,
So what do you want on yours—a lot of pinko longhairs, or
    red-blooded athaletes and drum majorettes?
Another thing, now every autumn it's like the coach had to
    open up a *new* factory,
But get rid of the classics and he can play his stars year
    after year until they're ready for the glue factory,

Because they can never graduate, but no crowd of self-
    appointed reformers can raise a nasty aroma,
Because the reason they can never graduate is there won't
    be anybody left who can write the Latin for their
    diploma.
So now let's all go to the Victory Prom
And join in singing Alma Mom.

---

## MY MY

### 1. MY DREAM

Here is a dream.
It is my dream—
My own dream—
I dreamt it.
I dreamt that my hair was kempt,
Then I dreamt that my true love unkempt it.

### 2. MY CONSCIENCE

I could of
If I would of,
But I shouldn't,
So I couldn't.

# I CAN'T HAVE A MARTINI, DEAR,
## BUT YOU TAKE ONE
### or
## ARE YOU GOING TO SIT THERE
### GUZZLING ALL NIGHT?

Come, spread foam rubber on the floor,
And sawdust and excelsior;
Soundproof the ceiling and the wall,
Unwind the clock within the hall,
Muffle in cotton wool the knell
Of doorbell and of decibel.
Ye milkman and ye garbage man,
Clink not the bottle, clash not the can;
Ye census taker, pass on by,
And Fuller Brush man, draw not nigh;
Street cleaner, do not splash or sprinkle;
Good Humor man, forbear to tinkle;
Ye Communists, overt or crypto-,
Slink past this shuttered house on tiptoe,
And cat, before you seek admittance,
Put sneakers on yourself and kittens;
Let even congressmen fall quiet,
For Chloë is on her latest diet,
And when Chloë is straightening out her curves
She's a sensitive bundle of quivering nerves.
Me you will find it useless to quiz
On what her latest diet is,
So rapidly our Chloë passes
From bananas to wheat germ and molasses.
First she will eat but chops and cheese,
Next, only things that grow on trees,
Now buttermilk, now milk that's malted,
And saccharin, and salt de-salted,
Salads with mineral oil and lemon in,
Repugnant even to palates feminine,
Lean fish, and fowl as gaunt as avarice,
And haggard haggis and curds cadaverous.
Today may bring gluten bread and carrots,

Tomorrow the eggs of penguins or parrots,
Because Chloë's dietetic needs
Shift with each article she reads.
But whatever her diet, from whence or whither,
When Chloë's on it, there's no living with her.

---

## I'LL EAT MY SPLIT-LEVEL TURKEY
## IN THE BREEZEWAY

A lady I know disapproves of the vulgarization of Christmas;
   she believes that Christmas should be governed purely
   by spiritual and romantic laws;
She says all she wants for Christmas is no more suggestive
   songs about Santa Claus.
Myself, I am more greedy if less cuddle-y,
And being of '02 vintage I am perforce greedy fuddy-duddily,
So my own Christmas could be made glad
Less by the donation of anything new than just by the re-
   turn of a few things I once had.
Some people strive for gracious living;
I have recurrent dreams of spacious living.
Not that I believe retrogression to be the be-all and the end-
   all,
Not that I wish to spend the holidays sitting in a Turkish
   corner smoking Sweet Caps and reading *Le Rouge et le
   Noir* by Stendhal,
Nor do I long for a castle with machicolations,
But I would like a house with a porte-cochere so the guests
   wouldn't get wet if it rained the evening of my party
   for my rich relations.
Also, instead of an alcove I'd like a dining room that there
   wasn't any doubt of,
And a bathtub that you didn't have to send $7.98 to Wis-
   consin for a device that enables you to hoist yourself
   out of,

And if there is one thought at which every cockle of my
    heart perks up and warms,
It is that of an attic in which to pile old toys and magazines
    and fancy dress costumes and suitcases with the handle
    off and dressmaker's forms.
I'd like a house full of closets full of shelves,
And above all, a house with lots of rooms all with doors that
    shut so that every member of the family could get off
    alone by themselves.
Please find me such a relic, dear Santa Claus, and when
    you've done it,
Please find me an old-fashioned cook and four old-fashioned
    maids at $8.00 a week and a genial wizard of a handy-
    man to run it.

---

## EXIT, PURSUED BY A BEAR

Chipmunk chewing the Chippendale,
Mice on the Meissen shelf,
Pigeon stains on the Aubusson,
Spider lace on the Delf.

Squirrel climbing the Sheraton,
Skunk on the Duncan Phyfe,
Silverfish in the Gobelins
And the calfbound volumes of *Life*.

Pocks on the pink Picasso,
Dust on the four Cézannes,
Kit on the keys of the Steinway,
Cat on the Louis Quinze.

Rings on the Adam mantel
From a thousand bygone thirsts,
Mold on the Henry Millers
And the Ronald Firbank firsts.

The lion and the lizard
No heavenly harmonies hear
From the high-fidelity speaker
Concealed behind the Vermeer.

Jamshid squats in a cavern
Screened by a waterfall,
Catered by Heinz and Campbell,
And awaits the fireball.

---

## A BRIEF GUIDE TO RHYMING,
### or
## HOW BE THE LITTLE BUSY DOTH?

English is a language than which none is sublimer,
But it presents certain difficulties for the rhymer.
There are no rhymes for orange or silver
Unless liberties you pilfer.
I was once slapped by a young lady named Miss Goringe,
And the only reason I was looking at her that way, she repre-
     sented a rhyme for orange.
I suggest that some painter do a tormented mural
On the perversity of the English plural,
Because perhaps the rhymer's greatest distress
Is caused by the letter s.
Oh, what a tangled web the early grammarians spun!
The singular verb has an s and the singular noun has none.
The rhymer notes this fact and ponders without success on it,
And moves on to find that his plural verb has dropped the s
     and his plural noun has grown an s on it.
Many a budding poet has abandoned his career
Unable to overcome this problem: that while the ear hears,
     the ears hear.
Yet he might have had the most splendiferous of careers

If only the *s*'s came out even and he could tell us what his
    ears hears.
However, I am happy to say that out from the bottom of this
    Pandora's box there flew a butterfly, not a moth,
The darling, four-letter word d-o-t-h, which is pronounced
    duth, although here we pronounce it doth.
Pronounce? Let jubilant rhymers pronounce it loud and clear,
Because when they can't sing that their ear hear they can
    legitimately sing that their ear doth hear.

---

## IF FUN IS FUN, ISN'T THAT ENOUGH?

Child, the temptation please resist
To deify the humorist.
Simply because we're stuck with solons
Whose minds resemble lazy colons,
Do not assume our current jesters
Are therefore Solomons and Nestors.
Because the editorial column
Is ponderously trite and solemn
Don't think the wisdom of the ages
Awaits you in the comic pages.
There is no proof that Plato's brain
Weighed less than that of Swift or Twain.
If funny men are sometimes right
It's second guessing, not second sight;
They apply their caustic common sense
After, and not before, events.
Since human nature's a *fait accompli*
They puncture it regularly and promptly.
Some are sophisticates, some earthy,
And none are totally trustworthy;
They'll sell their birthright every time
To make a point or turn a rhyme.
This motto, child, is my bequest:
There's many a false word spoken in jest.

# NATURE-WALKS
## or
# NOT TO MENTION A DOPPING OF SHELDRAKES

### 1. THE SQUID

What happy appellations these
Of birds and beasts in companies!
A shrewdness of apes, a sloth of bears,
A sculk of foxes, a huske of hares.
An exaltation 'tis of larks,
And possibly a grin of sharks,
But I declare a squirt of squid
I should not like to be amid,
Though bachelors claim that a cloud of sepia
Makes a splendid hiding place in Leap Year.

### 2. THE OSTRICH

The ostrich roams the great Sahara.
Its mouth is wide, its neck is narra.
It has such long and lofty legs,
I'm glad it sits to lay its eggs.

### 3. THE PRAYING MANTIS

From whence arrived the praying mantis?
From outer space, or lost Atlantis?
I glimpse the grim, green metal mug
That masks this pseudo-saintly bug,
Orthopterous, also carnivorous,
And faintly whisper, Lord deliver us.

### 4. THE ABOMINABLE SNOWMAN

I've never seen an abominable snowman,
I'm hoping not to see one,
I'm also hoping, if I do,
That it will be a wee one.

## 5. THE MANATEE

The manatee is harmless
And conspicuously charmless.
Luckily the manatee
Is quite devoid of vanity.

## 6. THE SQUAB

Toward a better world I contribute my modest smidgin;
I eat the squab, lest it become a pigeon.

---

## UP FROM THE EGG:
## THE CONFESSIONS OF A NUTHATCH AVOIDER

Bird watchers top my honors list.
I aimed to be one, but I missed.
Since I'm both myopic and astigmatic,
My aim turned out to be erratic,
And I, bespectacled and binocular,
Exposed myself to comment jocular.
We don't need too much birdlore, do we,
To tell a flamingo from a towhee;
Yet I cannot, and never will,
Unless the silly birds stand still.
And there's no enlightenment so obscure
As ornithological literature.
Is yon strange creature a common chickadee,
Or a migrant *alouette* from Picardy?
You rush to consult your Nature guide
And inspect the gallery inside,
But a bird in the open never looks
Like its picture in the birdie books—
Or if it once did, it has changed its plumage,
And plunges you back into ignorant gloomage.

That is why I sit here growing old by inches,
Watching the clock instead of finches,
But I sometimes visualize in my gin
The Audubon that I audubin.

---

## THERE'LL ALWAYS BE A WAR
## BETWEEN THE SEXES
### or
## A WOMAN CAN BE SOMETIMES PLEASED,
## BUT NEVER SATISFIED

I used to know a breadwinner named Mr. Purefoy who was
    far from the top of the heap,
Indeed he could only be called a breadwinner because he had
    once won half a loaf of whole wheat in the Irish Sweep.
His ambition was feverish,
His industry was eager-beaverish,
His wife was a thrifty helpmeet who got full value for every
    disbursement,
Yet their financial status showed no betterment, just perpetual
    worsement.
The trouble with these two was that they dissipated their
    energies,
They didn't play the percenages.
If he got angry at a slovenly, insolent waiter when they were
    dining in town
She would either bury her face in the menu or try to calm
    him down.
If she got angry at the woman in front of her at the movies
    and loudly suggested that she push her hat a little lower,
He pretended he didn't know her.
He defended his unappreciative employer against her loyal
    wifely ire,
And when he got burned up about the bills from the friendly
    exorbitant little grocer around the corner she tried to put
    out the fire.

One day they had a thought sublime,
They thought, Let's both get mad at the same person or situation at the same time.
I don't know about Mars, but Earth has not a denizen,
Who can withstand the wrath of a husband and wife being wrathful in unison.
To be said, little remains;
Only that after they merged their irascibility, it required the full time of three Certified Public Accountants and one Certified Private Accountant to keep track of their capital gains.

---

## POSIES FROM A SECOND CHILDHOOD
### or
### HARK HOW GAFFER DO CHAFFER

#### DADDY'S HOME, SEE YOU TOMORROW

I always found my daughter's beaux
Invisible as the emperor's clothes,
And I could hear of them no more
Than the slamming of an auto door.
My chicks would then slip up to roost;
They were, I finally deduced,
Concealing tactfully, pro tem,
Not beaux from me but me from them.

#### THE ABSENTEES

The healthy human child will keep
Away from home, except to sleep.
Were it not for the common cold
Our young we never would behold.

Mr. Longfellow spoke only part of the truth,
Though a fatherly poet of pre-eminent rank;
A girl's will is the twister's will.
It can drive a parent through a two-inch plank.

## PREFACE TO THE PAST

Time all of a sudden tightens the tether,
And the outspread years are drawn together.
How confusing the beams from memory's lamp are;
One day a bachelor, the next a grampa.
What is the secret of the trick?
How did I get so old so quick?
Perhaps I can find by consulting the files
How step after step added up to miles.
I was sauntering along, my business minding,
When suddenly struck by affection blinding,
Which led to my being a parent nervous
Before they invented the diaper service.
I found myself in a novel pose,
Counting infant fingers and toes.
I tried to be as wise as Diogenes
In the rearing of my two little progenies,
But just as I hit upon wisdom's essence
They changed from infants to adolescents.
I stood my ground, being fairly sure
That one of these days they must mature,
So when I was properly humbled and harried,
They did mature, and immediately married.
Now I'm counting, the cycle being complete,
The toes on my children's children's feet.
Here lies my past, good-by I have kissed it;
Thank you, kids, I wouldn't have missed it.

## BIRTHDAY ON THE BEACH

At another year
I would not boggle,
Except that when I jog
I joggle.

---

## CROSSING THE BORDER

Senescence begins
And middle age ends
The day your descendants
Outnumber your friends.

# ABOUT THE AUTHOR

Ogden Nash was born August 19, 1902, at Rye, New York. He has ten thousand cousins in North Carolina, his great-great-grandfather was revolutionary governor of the state, and the latter's brother, General Francis Nash, gave his name to Nashville, Tennessee.

He entered Harvard in the class of 1924 but left after one year. This was his own idea and not the dean's and he has affidavits to prove it. Nash spent a year as an instructor in St. George's School, Newport, Rhode Island, and to continue in his own inimitable manner: ". . . lost my entire nervous system carving lamb for a table of fourteen-year-olds. Came to New York to make my fortune as a bond salesman and in two years sold one bond—to my godmother. However, I saw a lot of good movies. Next went to work writing cards for Barron Collier. After two years of that I landed in the advertising department of Doubleday Page. That was 1925 and I doubledayed until the beginning of 1931. Then joined the editorial staff of *The New Yorker.*"

Since leaving the staff of *The New Yorker,* Nash has devoted most of his time to writing. After one unsuccessful tour in Hollywood, he collaborated with S. J. Perelman and the late Kurt Weill on the hit musical comedy *One Touch of Venus.* Since the beginning of the thirties, his poems have appeared in eleven published volumes and in well over a score of magazines across the nation. Even in the face of his proliferation, poetic idiosyncrasies and verbal pyrotechnics, Nash, Clifton Fadiman has pointed out, "is no mere oddity." From the togetherness pages of *McCall's* to the elegance of *Vogue* to the sophistication of *The New Yorker,* "what brings Nash home to our hearts is not his restatement of the familiar matter of poetry, but his statement of the familiar matter of daily living. . . . Nash is a true household poet in that he really understands the joys and sorrows of domestic life. He does not, like the folksy household poet, sentimentalize them. He is always the understanding host, never the unwelcome Guest."

The ubiquitous Nashean voice long ago reached England, where he is acclaimed not "merely as a funny man," but as a poet with "a Democritean streak which entitles him to the respect due to a philosopher, albeit a laughing one." At the heart of Nash's comic talent lies a patented point of view that has long since reduced his countless imitators to the rank of poetasters. Whether lauded as our best literary comedian since Will Rogers, the wise Shakespearean fool or the prophet with the tickling harpoon, Nash lances "the ideas, the foibles, the little vanities and the big issues, the inconsistencies and capriciousness of contemporary life," accomplishing so often what only real poetry can—allowing the reader to discover what he didn't know he already knew or felt.

Ogden Nash continues to delight and his most recent book, a long Christmas poem entitled *Santa Go Home*, struck a responsive chord in millions of Santaphobes—especially parents.